AF370788

# COMPANY K

## LECTOR HOUSE PUBLIC DOMAIN WORKS

This book is a result of an effort made by Lector House towards making a contribution to the preservation and repair of original classic literature. The original text is in the public domain in the United States of America, and possibly other countries depending upon their specific copyright laws.

In an attempt to preserve, improve and recreate the original content, certain conventional norms with regard to typographical mistakes, hyphenations, punctuations and/or other related subject matters, have been corrected upon our consideration. However, few such imperfections might not have been rectified as they were inherited and preserved from the original content to maintain the authenticity and construct, relevant to the work. The work might contain a few prior copyright references as well as page references which have been retained, wherever considered relevant to the part of the construct. We believe that this work holds historical, cultural and/or intellectual importance in the literary works community, therefore despite the oddities, we accounted the work for print as a part of our continuing effort towards preservation of literary work and our contribution towards the development of the society as a whole, driven by our beliefs.

We are grateful to our readers for putting their faith in us and accepting our imperfections with regard to preservation of the historical content. We shall strive hard to meet up to the expectations to improve further to provide an enriching reading experience.

Though, we conduct extensive research in ascertaining the status of copyright before redeveloping a version of the content, in rare cases, a classic work might be incorrectly marked as not-in-copyright. In such cases, if you are the copyright holder, then kindly contact us or write to us, and we shall get back to you with an immediate course of action.

### HAPPY READING!

# COMPANY K

## DANIEL P. SMITH

ISBN: 978-93-5614-430-9

Published: 1885

© 2022
LECTOR HOUSE LLP

LECTOR HOUSE LLP
E-MAIL: lectorpublishing@gmail.com

# COMPANY K

## FIRST ALABAMA REGIMENT,
## OR
## THREE YEARS IN
## THE CONFEDERATE SERVICE

BY

## DANIEL P. SMITH.

1885.

# CONTENTS

## CHAPTER XII.

# INTRODUCTORY.

The First Alabama Regiment of Infantry was organized under the Act of the Legislature authorizing the enlistment of troops for twelve months. Three companies were raised in Barbour county by Capts. Alpheus Baker, John Clark and Jere. Williams; two in Pike, by Capts. Augustus Owen and Dawson; one in Wilcox, by Capt. I. G. W. Steadman; one in Tallapoosa, by Capt. J. D. Meadows; one in Talladega, by Capt. L. F. Johnson; one in Lowndes, by Capt. J. D. Conyers; and one in Mobile, by Capt. Ben. Lane Posey. The companies were ordered to rendezvous at Pensacola, for the purpose of relieving the independent companies at that time occupying the captured forts, Barrancas and McRae, and the navy yard. About February 10, 1861, the first companies arrived at Pensacola, and the others rapidly followed. It was not until April that the regimental organization was completed, by the election and appointment of the following officers: Colonel, Henry D. Clayton; Lieutenant-colonel, I. G. W. Steadman; Major, Jere. Williams; Quartermaster, Capt. L. F. Johnson; Commissary, Capt. Henry Shorter; Adjutant, S. H. Dent; Surgeon, J. D. Caldwell, M. D.; Assistant-Surgeon, Walter Curry, M. D.

Soon after its organization, by Act of the State Legislature, but with its own consent, the regiment was mustered into the service of the Confederate States, and was assigned to duty in Fort Barrancas and the heavy batteries along the shore of the bay. Many of these batteries were thrown up by the men of the First Alabama, who, thus early in the war, were accustomed to the use of entrenching tools. Military instruction was not neglected; and, while industriously wielding pick and shovel, the men were thoroughly drilled, both as heavy artillery and infantry.

A portion of the regiment was engaged in the fight on Santa Rosa Island, and then the whole regiment served in the batteries during the bombardments of the 23d of November, 1861, and the 1st of January, 1862. For its gallantry on these occasions it received complimentary mention in Gen. Bragg's orders.

At the close of twelve months' service, the regiment was called upon to re-enlist for the war, and seven companies promptly responded. Capts. Baker's, Clark's and Posey's companies were mustered out, and were replaced by Capt. Knowles' company, from Macon county; Capt. William Pruitt's, from Barbour; and Capt. J. F. Whitfield's, from Autauga. The regiment was reorganized by the election of the following officers; Colonel, I. G. W. Steadman; Lieutenant-colonel, M. B. Locke; Major, S. L. Knox; Adjutant, S. D. Steadman; Quartermaster, Capt. Duncan Carmichael; Surgeon, Dr. Schackelford (afterwards succeeded by Dr. Hamilton). The companies were commanded respectively as follows: Co. A, Capt. J. D. Meadows; Co. B, Capt. Ramsey; Co. C, Capt. Stubbs; Co. D, Capt. R. H. Isbell; Co. E, Capt.

Woods; Co. F, Capt. Williams; Co. G, Capt. Riley; Co. H, Capt. Knowles; Co. I, Capt. William Pruitt; Co. K, Capt. John F. Whitfield.

In the following pages will be found a sketch of the services of Co. K, of Autauga county. Although the author makes no higher pretence than to be a company historian, yet he has embodied in the story all the facts connected with the history of the other companies, and of the regiment as a whole, that were in his possession. From the day that Co. K joined the regiment, in March, 1862, until the surrender of Gen. Joseph E. Johnston, it shared in all the toils, privations and dangers of the gallant "First," and its history is indissolubly blended with it. Therefore, with the kindest feelings, the writer dedicates this little work, not only to the members of Co. K, but to all his comrades in the

Fɪʀsᴛ Aʟᴀʙᴀᴍᴀ.

# CHAPTER I.

Organization of the John Gill Shorter Artillery—Change of Destination—At Island 10—Roll of Company K—Mysteries of the Cuisine—A Shameful Waste.


In February, 1862, John F. Whitfield, Esq., obtained the authority to recruit one of the three companies necessary to complete the reorganization of the First Alabama Regiment, C. S. A., serving at that time as heavy artillery at Pensacola, Fla. Meeting with Merrill E. Pratt, Esq., of Prattville, he proposed to that gentleman to raise one-half the company, he himself expecting to bring thirty or forty men into the field. Mr. Pratt was thinking, at this time, of joining another regiment with a small squad of men, who desired to be with him in the army, but, seeing now a wider field for usefulness, he accepted the proposal. In a few days, through his personal influence and popularity, he enrolled the names of nearly fifty volunteers, including some of the best men in Autauga county, and, had he not been restricted by the terms of his agreement with Capt. Whitfield, he could, without difficulty, have recruited a full company. On the 7th of March, Lieut. Pratt and his men proceeded to Montgomery, and, on the following day, were mustered into the service of the Confederacy, styling themselves, in honor of the Governor of the State, the "John Gill Shorter Artillery." John F. Whitfield was elected Captain; M. E. Pratt, First Lieutenant; Dixon S. Hall, Second Lieutenant, Jr.; and Charles E. Tuttle, Orderly Sergeant. The second lieutenancy was left vacant, to be filled by the squad of men Capt. Whitfield still expected to secure. For the failure of these men to report, Capt. Whitfield was in no manner responsible, he acting throughout in good faith. No officer had more the confidence and affection of his men than Capt. Whitfield, and this esteem he retained from first to last.

While in Montgomery, enameled cloth knapsacks and haversacks, and cedar canteens, were issued to the men, but they provided their own uniforms, no two of which were alike.

When enrolled the men expected to go to Pensacola, but upon arriving in Montgomery, it was learned that the regiment had left that place for New Madrid, Mo., a fortified post on the Mississippi River. As this change in destination, from a warm to a cold climate, and from garrison to field duty, necessitated a change in clothing, leave of absence for two days was given the members of the company to return home and make needed preparations. There was a general cutting down in the amount of *impedimenta*, though most of the men loaded themselves with twice the amount that could be carried on a march.

On the morning of March 10th, the company reassembled in Montgomery, and, under the command of Lieut. Hall, started for Memphis. Monday night they camped at Atlanta, not being able to proceed farther on account of the crowded trains. It was not till Wednesday noon that the company reached Memphis. The regiment was just leaving the city by the boat, and could not wait for the company to join; Lieut. Hall, however, reported, and received orders to proceed by the steamer "Republic," which left the next day at 5 P. M. Thursday night the boat reached Fort Pillow, where it was learned that New Madrid had been evacuated, and that the First Alabama had been ordered to Island No. 10. Friday evening the "Republic" arrived at Tiptonville, and the men disembarked; but, the boat being detained, they slept on board that night. Saturday they again landed, and marched across from Tiptonville to Island No. 10, a distance of six miles. The regiment was found encamped without tents in a newly-cleared field, and the company, thus early in its service, began roughing it. It was not till the 18th that they received any tents; they then were moved into a wood, some three-quarters of a mile from the river. On the 25th the camp was again moved, and tents pitched in regulation order in an open field in the rear of Batteries Nos. 5 and 6; a camp guard was detailed, and the military routine of guard-mounting, drill and dress-parade began.

Capt. Whitfield and Lieut. Pratt arrived on the 18th, receiving a hearty welcome. There now being no hope of the other squad reporting, it was decided that Lieut. Pratt should return home and recruit the company to its full strength.

Lieut. Dixon S. Hall was promoted to the second lieutenancy, and Orderly Sergt. C. E. Tuttle, who had ably performed his duties and looked after the comfort of the men, was made junior second lieutenant. The following is the roll of the company, as it stood at that time:—

*Captain*, John F. Whitfield.

*First Lieutenant*, Merrill E. Pratt.

*Second Lieutenant*, Dixon S. Hall.

*Second Lieutenant, Jr.*, Charles E. Tuttle.

*Orderly Sergeant*, Norman Cameron.

*Second Sergeant*, A. J. Thompson.

*Third Sergeant*, J. C. Rodgers.

*Fourth Sergeant*, A. J. Merritt.

*Fifth Sergeant*, E. T. Sears.

*First Corporal*, John Williamson.

*Second Corporal*, W. L. Ellis.

*Third Corporal*, J. M. Royals.

*Fourth Corporal*, W. H. Hutchinson.

*Privates.*

| | |
|---|---|
| N. K. Adams, | E. L. Averheart, |
| O. M. Blaylock, | G. R. Bledsoe, |

| | |
|---|---|
| A. P. Brown, | C. W. Brown, |
| E. F. Brown, | J. W. Cook, |
| W. A. Dennis, | J. H. Durden, |
| W. Farmer, | John Frank, Jr., |
| Wm. H. Fay, | J. A. Fergerson, |
| John Griffin, | M. M. Hancock, |
| Elijah Hearn, | G. W. Hearn, |
| J. C. Hearn, | J. W. Hearndon, |
| J. G. Holston, | Joseph Hurd, |
| J. W. Killough, | J. M. May, |
| C. J. Moncrief, | W. L. Moncrief, |
| Daniel P. Smith, | J. F. Smith, |
| Mac. A. Smith, | Junius Robinson, |
| J. L. Robinson, | C. H. Royals, |
| G. H. Royals, | J. D. Rice, |
| T. J. Roe, | J. G. Tarleton, |
| J. S. Tunnell, | Joseph Tunnell, |

Fletcher Wilkins.

Total, 4 commissioned officers, 9 non-commissioned officers and 39 privates.

W. H. Hutchinson was soon after detailed as a member of the drum corps, and O. M. Blaylock was appointed corporal in his stead. Joseph Hurd was detailed at the same time as fifer. All the above were present for duty, except Private Griffin, who received a furlough when he enlisted, and reported to Capt. Isbell after the surrender of the Island. Muskets were not issued to Co. K for two weeks after their arrival, but details for fatigue and guard duty were made after a few days. When Capt. Rucker's company was relieved at Battery No. 1, on the third or fourth day of the siege, a detail of sixty men from the First Alabama was ordered there, with daily relief. Co. K furnished four or five men of this detail.

The men were quickly initiated into the mysteries of the *cuisine*, and from the first day some were quite good cooks, while others made most amusing blunders. A camp-kettle, half full of rice, was a source of much worry to an amateur who attempted to boil it—there were not enough utensils in the company to hold South Carolina's favorite dish as it swelled in the pot. Commissary stores were plentiful, and there was a shameful waste. Fresh beef was hauled off and buried by the wagon load; barrels of corned beef remained untouched in the camp; while rice, flour, molasses and sugar were issued in larger quantities than could possibly be eaten. These were the last days of the "Flush times of the First Alabama."

On the 30th of March, Lieut. Pratt and Corp. Ellis left for Alabama to enlist recruits. About the same time Privates M. A. Smith and J. L. Robinson were honorably discharged on account of physical disability, and left for their homes.

# CHAPTER II.

Bombardment and Capture of Island No. 10—The Batteries—At Rucker's Battery—Canal Cutting—A Night Attack—Running the Gauntlet—An Unfinished Meal—The Attempted Evacuation—Retreat to Tiptonville—Mackall's Order—The Surrender—Across Reel-Foot River.

Island No. 10 is, or was, in the Mississippi River, opposite the boundary-line between Kentucky and Tennessee. The river approaches the island in nearly a southerly direction, then runs to the northwest about twelve miles to New Madrid, where it makes a semi-circular sweep, and takes its course to the southeast for sixteen miles to Tiptonville, Tenn., forming a great horseshoe bend of six miles in width, and opening to the southeast. Across this opening, a few miles to the eastward, is Reel-Foot River or bayou, emptying into the Mississippi below Tiptonville; in high water expanding into a lake, and connecting with the Mississippi above Island No. 10, cutting off all approach except by boats.

At the beginning of the bombardment, Gen. McCown was in command of the Confederate forces, augmented, by the evacuation of New Madrid, to some ten or twelve thousand men. More than half these troops were, however, withdrawn about the last of March. The batteries, which had been ably planned, but imperfectly constructed, under direction of Capt. Harris, of the Engineer Corps, contained forty-four guns, mostly 32 and 42 pound smooth-bores, with a few 64-pounders and one or two 100-pound rifles. Twenty-seven guns, not mounted, were scattered along the river bank and on the Island. The batteries were distributed as follows: On the Tennessee bank of the river were six—No. 1 (Rucker's), six guns; No. 2, four guns; No. 3, three guns; No. 4, four guns; No. 5, two guns; No. 6, seven guns; total, twenty-seven. On the Island were four batteries—No. 1, six guns; No. 2, four guns; No. 3, five guns; No. 4, two guns; total, seventeen. A floating battery—the old Algiers floating dock—was moored to the left bank of the Island; and on the deck of this nondescript craft, wholly unprotected, were eight guns.

The enemy, upon the evacuation of New Madrid, established batteries there and soon after at Point Pleasant, opposite Tiptonville—thus cutting off approach to the island by river. Boats made a landing at Tiptonville and—when it became too warm there—at a point just below, and thus communication was kept up till the gunboats ran the Island 10 batteries, a few days before the surrender.

On the morning of March 15th the Federal fleet arrived from above, and opened fire upon the Confederate works. There were seven iron-clads: the "Benton," "Louisville," "Carondelet," "Conestoga," "Pittsburgh," "St. Louis" and

"Mound City," armed with ten heavy guns each, and eight mortar-boats, each carrying one thirteen-inch mortar. Their fire concentrated on Rucker's and the Island batteries, was continued all day and slowly on Sunday, the 16th. Monday morning the iron-clads, lashed three together, dropped down the river, stern foremost, to within a mile and a half of Rucker's Battery and anchored. They maintained a heavy fire all day, throwing, with the mortar fleet, 1,350 shot and shell, of which 1,000 were hurled at Capt. Rucker's guns and 350 at the Island. There was no one hurt on the Island, though there were many narrow escapes. At Battery No. 1, on the main land, a shot passed through the parapet, dismounting a gun, killing Lieut. Clark, of Capt. Rucker's company, and wounding several men. These were the only casualties during the siege.

Elcon Jones, of the Signal Corps, was stationed at Rucker's Battery. During the day his signal-flag was twice shot from his hand. In one instance he was transmitting a message, and he picked up the flag and continued his communication without missing a word. He was afterwards complimented in general orders by Gen. Beauregard and promoted.

The Confederate artillery practice was very good; the iron-clads were repeatedly hit, and before night they hauled off, continuing their fire with their long-range rifles. One shot struck the "Benton," passed through her iron-clad side into the Captain's cabin, bounded from the floor to the ceiling and landed on the table. The dismounted gun at Battery 1 was placed in position again that night, not having been seriously damaged.

Tuesday the bombardment was resumed, but the fleet did not come within good range of the Confederate smooth-bores, and our fire was, in consequence, slack. Capt. Rucker's company, exhausted by its severe labors, was relieved by the First Alabama. The river continuing to rise, the working of the guns in Battery No. 1 was rendered difficult, if not impossible, by the water, which was two feet deep on the platforms. All the powder and shell had to be removed from the magazine, and, without other protection than a tarpaulin, stowed in an angle of the breastworks. On rainy days some of the guards would creep under the tarpaulin, propping it up with a handspike so as to get air; but this improvised tent would invariably attract the enemy's attention, and a shell would go shrieking over, causing the hasty striking of the shelter. A deep slough connecting with Reel-Foot Bayou cut off all approach to this battery except in boats, and as the relief details had to be sent up after dark, a trip on stormy nights was attended with some risk. On one occasion a boat was carried by the swift current into the swamp and capsized; the crew were not rescued till daylight—passing the night, cold and wet, on stumps or driftwood.

In the meantime the enemy's engineers were clearing a channel, or canal, through the swamps and bayous on the west side of the river, from a point above the Island to one below, to enable them to get small transports below the batteries and to transport troops across the river and take the Confederates in the rear. But little digging was required, as the high stage of the river gave the necessary depth of water; but the trees had to be cut out of the way. The trees were felled, leaving the stumps just above the water. A cross-cut saw, forming the lower side of a triangular frame, was then pivoted by the upper angle to the stump, so as to swing freely—the blade of the saw being four feet below the surface of the water. Twenty men on a side operating this simple device could cut off a stump two feet in diameter in a few minutes. The canal was completed early in April, and several transports were at once sent through, arriving safely at New Madrid. As the gunboats were of too deep draught to use the canal, preparations were at once made to run one of them by the batteries, and, as a preliminary step, it was decided to spike the guns in the dangerous upper battery.

On the night of April 1st five boats were made ready with crews from the gunboats "Cincinnati," "St. Louis," "Benton," "Pittsburgh" and "Mound City," and volunteers from the Forty-Third Illinois Infantry, all under command of Col. Roberts. In each boat were twenty men, exclusive of officers. Every precaution was taken to insure secrecy; the oar-locks were muffled, and the expedition did not start till midnight, when all was quiet. The night was dark and stormy, and the only difficulty was in finding the battery; but a flash of lightning revealed its position as they got abreast, and a landing was effected without opposition. But two sentinels were on the battery; these fired their guns and ran back to the main guard, who were on the parapet of the breastwork in the rear. By the time the alarm was fairly given the enemy had spiked the guns and re-embarked. The successful termination of this attack was due largely to the fact that the battery being submerged except the parapet, there was no place for the guard immediately around the guns, though there was, undoubtedly, carelessness in not having more men on duty. A boat was despatched to camp with the alarm, and a fresh detachment of men was sent up. Co. K, prior to this event, had received no arms, but during the alarm a lot of old muskets and ten rounds of cartridges were distributed. Two of the guns were unspiked during the nights of the 2d and 3d.

The night of April 4th set in dark and threatening; in the midst of a terrific thunder-storm the long-roll sounded, and the battalion was hastily formed in line of battle in the rear of the batteries. Mingled with the almost continuous roll of the thunder was the roar of a heavy cannonade, while the lightning and the flashes of the guns, rendered more vivid by the intense darkness of the night, combined to render it a scene of wonderful grandeur. The firing continued but for a brief period, and quiet being restored, the men were dismissed to their quarters.

In the morning it was ascertained that the iron-clad "Carondelet," protected by barges of baled hay, had successfully run the batteries. She was first discovered by the sentinels at Rucker's Battery, who fired their muskets, giving the alarm. An attempt was made to use the two guns which had been unspiked, but the charges were damp, not having been drawn after the guns were unspiked, and they could not be fired.

During the 5th the fleet shelled the camp of the First Alabama and other regiments, but no one was hurt. The following night the enemy crossed a small force opposite New Madrid, and spiked the batteries of light artillery stationed there, but immediately retired.

Sunday, the 6th of April, was clear and pleasant, and passed quietly. At dress-parade the troops were ordered to be in readiness to march at the sounding of the long-roll. The signal came while the men were preparing or eating supper, and leaving everything—the tents standing, cooking utensils scattered around, in some cases the food half cooked in the kettles—the battalion of the First Alabama in camp, numbering about 325 men, formed on the parade-ground and marched to the general headquarters. About 350 of the regiment stationed on the Island, 60 at Battery No. 1 and a considerable number sick in camp were left behind.

The commander of the forces at this time was Gen. Mackall, Gen. McCown having been relieved April 1st. It was dark when the troops, about fifteen hundred in number, left headquarters, the First Alabama in the advance. After marching ten miles, the column was halted in the woods, and formed in line of battle about half a mile from the river and nearly opposite New Madrid. It soon began to rain, and as fires were not permitted, the condition of affairs was anything but pleasant. The object of the move was, ostensibly, to prevent a landing of the enemy, crossing from New Madrid. The night, however, passed without alarm, except a slight stir caused by pickets bringing in a prisoner. A heavy cannonade in the direction of Island No. 10 announced that another iron-clad had stolen by in the darkness. This vessel, it was afterwards learned, was the "Pittsburgh;" she was protected in the same way as the "Carondelet," and received no injury. Daybreak found the men cold, wet and hungry, many of them having eaten no supper. The wagons arrived about 7 o'clock; flour, bacon and cooking utensils were issued to the companies, and an attempt was made to prepare breakfast; but orders to resume the march compelled the men to leave the half-cooked meal on the coals. Information had been received that the Federal troops were crossing lower down the river, and that the garrison was in danger of being cut off. Many of the troops were unaccustomed to marching, and upon leaving camp had overburdened themselves with baggage. As a consequence, the road along which the men were hurried was strewn with every kind and description of apparel and not a few blankets. It was nearly dark when the command approached Tiptonville, and, making a detour, passed around and below it. That landing was already in possession of the enemy, and a force of their cavalry were following close in the rear of the retreating Confederates, picking up stragglers. While opposite Tiptonville there was an alarm, and the column was halted and brought to a front; but no attack was made, and the march was resumed. About three-quarters of a mile below Tiptonville the command was formed in line of battle, and there remained all night, the men sleeping in ranks, with their arms by their sides. Gens. Gantt and Walker, who had been stationed opposite New Madrid, had retired with our command, and the combined force numbered between 2,000 and 3,000 men.

At 11 o'clock, Monday night, Gen. Mackall arranged terms for the surrender of his army, but the soldiers were not made aware of it until the next morning, otherwise many would have made their escape. The universal feeling among men and officers was, that the surrender was utterly uncalled for, and that the greater portion of the force could have been safely taken out while a few men held Gen. Pope's army in check. Many denounced Gen. Mackall as a traitor, and asserted that the surrender had been arranged several days before. While this report was wholly without foundation, yet of his incapacity no one who was present could have any doubt. Gen. McCown was removed by Gen. Beauregard because, after the fall of New Madrid, he had pronounced the position at Island No. 10 untenable, and Gen. Mackall was ordered there, with instructions to hold it at all hazards until further orders. On the morning after the gunboat "Carondelet" passed the batteries, he issued the following address to the troops:—

HEADQUARTERS, ISLAND No. 10,<br>April 5, 1862.

SOLDIERS:—We are strangers—the commander to the commanded, and each to the other. Let me tell you who I am.

I am a general made by Beauregard—a general selected by Gens. Beauregard and Bragg for this command when they knew it was in peril. They have known me for twenty years; together we have stood in the fields of Mexico. Give them your confidence! Give it me when I have earned it!

Soldiers! the Mississippi Valley is entrusted to your courage, to your discipline, to your patience. Exhibit the vigilance and coolness of last night, and hold it!

(Signed)                                    WILLIAM D. MACKALL,
*Brig.-Gen. Commanding.*

Gen. Beauregard, in a communication published since the close of the war, expressed himself as satisfied with Gen. Mackall's performance of the trust, but his troops saw only a series of blunders.

Gen. Mackall surrendered 3,000 men, 4,000 stand of arms, 75 siege guns and 24 pieces of light artillery. The enemy captured four transports afloat, and two transports and the gunboat "Grampus" which had been scuttled, and a considerable amount of stores and ammunition.

The following are the members of Co. K who were surrendered at Tiptonville: Capt. J. F. Whitfield, Lieut. D. S. Hall, Lieut. C. E. Tuttle, Sergts. Thompson, Rodgers, Merritt and Sears, Corps. Williamson and Blaylock, Privates Adams, Bledsoe, C. W. Brown, Cook, Dennis, Farmer, Frank, Fay, Hurd, Killough, May, C. H. Royals, Rice, Roe, D. P. Smith, J. S. Tunnell and Josiah Tunnell; total, 3 officers and 23 enlisted men. The commissioned officers were sent to Columbus, Ohio, and afterwards transferred to Johnson's Island; the enlisted men were sent to Camp Butler, near Springfield, Ill. Several of the company were sick, and, with their attendants, were taken prisoners at the camp or in the hospital, viz.: Privates A. P. Brown, E. F. Brown, Fergerson, J. C. Hearn, Hearndon, C. J. Moncrief, W. L. Moncrief, J. F. Smith and Tarleton; total, 9. These were sent to Madison, Wis., and afterwards transferred to Camp Douglas, Chicago, Ill. J. F. Smith, mentioned above, started from the Island 10 camp with the company, but was attacked with measles, and was sent back to the hospital. Several hundred of the troops escaped across Reel-Foot River by wading and by boats. Among these were the following members of Co. K: Sergt. Norman Cameron, Corp. J. M. Royals, Privates Averheart, Durden,

Hancock, Hutchinson, Elijah Hearn, George Hearn, Holston, Junius Robinson, G. H. Royals and Wilkins; total, 12. Some of these were on detail at Battery 1 and elsewhere, and others were on the sick-list when the company left camp.

The companies of the First Alabama stationed at the Island batteries were surrendered by direction of Gen. Mackall to Commodore Porter, Monday night, and were afterwards sent to Camp Butler, Ill.

# CHAPTER III.

Prison Life in 1862—In the Mud—Bivouac at New Madrid—A Friendly Irishman—At Camp Butler—Scant Water Supply—Escape of
Prisoners—An Astonished Sentinel—Playing Guard—Lost on the
Prairie—A Prisoner Shot—Health of the Camp—Mortality Sta-
tistics—Curious Phenomena—Death Visits the Company—Col.
Fundy in Command—Practical Jokes—Trinket Making—News
from Comrades—Homeward Bound—Arrival in Dixie.


At daybreak on Tuesday, April 8th, the retreating garrison were quietly aroused
from their leafy, but not otherwise romantic, couches in the woods below Tiptonville. It was a cold, cloudy morning, and the men, who had been without food or
fire for twenty-four hours, stood impatiently in line of battle eager for something
to be done that would warm up their chilled limbs and bodies. To continue the retreat, or to fight either would have been a welcome change, but the order that was
passed down the lines was received almost in a spirit of mutiny by both officers
and men. All knew that "Do not fire on the enemy" could mean nothing but surrender. Rations were served out, cooking utensils distributed, and fires built; but
while busy cooking the men were ordered to "fall in," "stack arms" and "march,"
and breakfast was abandoned or eaten half raw. Upon arriving at Tiptonville the
surrendered army was formed in close column, in an open field, and surrounded
by guards. The field had been cultivated in corn, the previous year, and though
the hollows between the rows might in dry weather, have offered rather tempting
couches, they were treacherous ones in a wet season, while the black swamp mud
was not conducive to cleanliness. During the day flour and bacon were served out,
and the men had plenty of time to cook and eat. With night came on a storm, and
the prisoners made such shelters as they could with fence rails and blankets. The
only fuel was that offered by fences, with the stumps of the newly cleared land for
*pieces de resistance.* Those who essayed the blanket shelters were roused by trick-
ling streams of water from above, to find themselves lying in ponds of water one
or two inches deep. Sounder sleepers would not awake till some rascal had filched
their blankets, and the fire-builders had stolen their rails. By midnight the majority
of the twenty-five hundred prisoners were packed, in circular groups, six or seven
deep, around the fires, which dotted the field, or were wandering disconsolately
from fire to fire hoping to find some place where a gleam of the flames could
be seen. The anathemas of the men were bestowed quite impartially upon the
weather, the Yankees and Gen. Mackall the Confederate Commander. Words and
invective were exhausted in showering curses upon the last. Had they not been
prisoners the discomforts of the night would have been of little moment, but under

the existing circumstances it was dismal beyond description. Day at last dawned, and the men were almost ready to welcome with a cheer the arrival of the transports, which were to take them away from such a mud-hole, even though it was to a military prison. The boats were small stern-wheelers and conveyed the men only to New Madrid, Mo., where they were landed in the mud. New Madrid mud is red, contrasting well with the Tiptonville black, and, as there was no opportunity for ablutions, mud and smoke soon rendered the Confederates as varied in hue as Indian braves. Abundant rations of hard tack, bacon and coffee were served out, and, although the storm had not ended, the situation was much more comfortable than during the preceding twenty-four hours. The officers were now separated from the enlisted men—something akin in pain to parting parents from children.

Thursday afternoon the prisoners were again embarked, and, under convoy, the boats steamed up the river. At dusk the fleet passed Island 10, stopping for a short time; the next morning Columbus was left behind, and by 10.30 A. M. a landing was made at Cairo. The prisoners were here transferred to close box-cars, which to sight and smell, bore evidence of having, very recently, been used to transport cattle. A bale of hay was rolled into each car, to serve—when spread over the floor—as seats and bedding. To secure the safety and welfare of the passengers one guard was placed in each car, and was not relieved till the train reached its destination. The sentinel in our car was an Irishman, a social, friendly fellow, considerate of the prisoners' feelings and reposing great confidence in their honor, which confidence was not abused. Probably his superiors would have been somewhat astonished at his ideas about guard duty, which were not those laid down in army regulations. Whenever the train stopped, even after nightfall, he would either allow some of the prisoners to jump out and fill their canteens, or go himself. During the night he handed his musket to one of the Confederates, laid down in the hay and went to sleep. His brother, the guard in the next car got uproariously drunk, and about midnight came stumbling into our car. He was so quarrelsome that we put him out, in a few minutes he was back, this time bringing his musket and threatening vengeance, but our slumbering guardian being aroused quieted him with a few words, more forcible than elegant, and sent him back to his post. Placed under a *quasi* parole of honor by the kindness of our Irish friend, not a prisoner attempted to escape from his car though there was abundant opportunity. In one village through which we passed in the night citizen's dress was offered to some of the men to enable them to escape if they so desired. The train reached Camp Butler, four miles from Springfield, Ill., Saturday afternoon, April 12th. In the surrounding fields patches of snow were still visible, but the camp itself was a mud-puddle. When we left Alabama, a month previous, the fruit trees were in blossom, planters were busy ploughing, and the air was mild and balmy; on our arrival at Island 10 it was cold and the trees were bare, the first signs of Spring appearing as we left; now, for the third time, we were to have wintry weather. There were at Camp Butler fifteen or eighteen hundred prisoners taken at Fort Donelson, these occupied eighteen out of the twenty barracks within the prison lines, two being used as hospitals. The new arrivals were ordered from the cars and marched to the parade ground for inspection; blankets were unrolled, knapsacks unstrapped and the persons of the prisoners searched for concealed weapons, but no money or valuables were taken. Some three hundred of the prisoners were then sent to the barracks, and to the remaining six or seven hundred were allotted tents, one to every six or eight men, boards were distributed for floors and before night the men were comfortably sheltered. The barracks were about sixty feet long by twenty wide, standing twenty feet apart, and were intended to accommodate one hundred men each. In front of the barracks—a street fifty feet wide intervening—the tents were pitched. Immediately to the rear of the line of tents was the guard and dead line; the dead line at the ends was within a few feet of the lines of barracks and tents and about two hundred feet to the rear of the barracks, thus enclosing in round numbers a parallelogram 800 feet long by 300 or 350 feet wide. As the warm weather came on, a second line of tents was pitched in the rear of the first and the crowded barracks relieved. The supply of water on our arrival was drawn from five or six wells within the enclosure; each barrack was supplied with a rope, and each mess used its own camp-kettle for a bucket, attaching it to the rope and drawing it up hand over hand. The scene around the wells was a lively one, especially just before the time for preparing meals. During the rainy season the supply of water in the wells was tolerably plentiful, though it would occasionally give out. By the first of May, however, the wells began to fail, and on May 7th it is recorded in the writer's diary: "Water is getting to be a luxury, the wells are exhausted before sunrise." After that time water was hauled from Sangamon river—about a mile distant—details of prisoners going with the wagons to fill up the hogsheads and barrels. It was esteemed a great privilege to go with the wagons as it gave opportunity to bathe and to gather mussels in the river. The fresh country air too was a wonderful contrast to the stifled atmosphere of the prison camp on a hot day. Outside the guard lines was another prison hospital, set apart for erysipelas cases, of which there were many among the prisoners. Its occupants burned in stripes with lunar caustic and painted with iodine, were a horribly grotesque crowd. Side by side with this hospital was the dead house, always tenanted with bodies waiting burial. At the head of the street, which separated the barracks and tents, was the "headquarters" of the Commandant of the post; at the other end of the street was the guard house with its dreaded "black hole," a cell without light or ventilation. In an addition to these buildings were the Commissary's, Quartermaster's and Sutler's stores, and the barracks for the guard.

When the Island No. 10 prisoners arrived the camp was not enclosed, and there had been in consequence many escapes. It was quite common to hear in the morning the announcement, "A squad of prisoners left for home last night." As calling the roll was entrusted to non-commissioned officers among the prisoners—there were no commissioned officers prisoners at Camp Butler—and as their reports were verified not oftener than once a week, several days were usually allowed to elapse before absentees were reported, thus giving them a fair start in the race for the Ohio or Mississippi Rivers. As many as nine broke through the guard lines in a single night; nor were escapes confined to the darkness, sometimes a break would be made in the broad daylight, and as the cavalry patrolled the lines during the day with sabres, the only risk was that of recapture. In one case, as the astonished sentinel saw prisoner after prisoner flitting by, he cried out, in accents of despair, "Corporal of the guard! corporal of the guard! run here quick, all the rebels are getting away!" These frequent escapes of prisoners soon led to more rigorous measures. Those recaptured were incarcerated in the black hole for a week or ten days; all prisoners were required to remain in their barracks from dusk until reveille, under penalty of being shot, and a board fence ten feet high was built around the camp. The fence, made chiefly by volunteers from among the prisoners, small wages being paid them, was completed early in May, and served to check the flight of the prisoners, though it did not prove an effectual barrier. Not many nights after its completion, during a storm, a party of four scaled it by aid of a short ladder they had constructed; a flash of lightning revealed them to the guard, who fired, but without effect. Some of the prisoners who worked on the fence, broke short the nails with which certain marked boards were fastened; making a dash for the fence one day they pulled off one of these planks, and three got through before the sentinel could fire. Two of the three were recaptured while running the gauntlet of a militia camp, just outside the enclosure and did penance in the "black hole," the third escaped. An attempt was made to tunnel out, but it was betrayed to Maj. Fundy, and stopped when the tunnel had nearly reached the fence; it was started from a freshly dug sink. Those engaged in it escaped punishment by pledging their word not to renew the work. The cavalry regiment guarding the camp having been relieved by ununiformed militia, a novel plan of escape was successfully tried. A lot of rusty muskets had been found in one of the barracks by the Fort Donelson prisoners on their arrival, these had been carefully concealed with a view that they might sometime be useful. After the wells began to fail, and before the hauling of water in wagons had been begun, squads of prisoners were allowed to go out with guards to neighborhood wells and fill buckets and canteens. Procuring or fixing up costumes sufficiently like those worn by the militia to be mistaken for them, and brightening up the old muskets so as to pass muster, some of the prisoners played the part of guards and escorted out several squads who did not return. Another scheme was successfully played on the militia, who were very ignorant, many being unable to read. Hospital attendants were given passes to cross and recross the guard lines, they giving their paroles not to escape; noting carefully those of the guards who read these passes equally well bottom or right side up, bogus passes were prepared, no attempt being made to imitate the writing of the Federal officials, and the guards passed the holders out. No less than thirty left in this manner before the imposture was detected. None of those under parole violated their pledges, nor were they in any way connected with the writing of the spurious passes, but they suffered, as all passes were revoked. The regulations were henceforth so stringent that but few were able to elude the vigilance of the guards. During the six months that elapsed from the arrival of the prisoners to their departure for exchange, 225 escaped from Camp Butler. Not all of these, however, got back to Dixie, quite a number being recaptured and sent to other prisons. Among those who escaped by bogus passes was John Frank, Jr.; starting for the Mississippi River, he, and one or two companions, lost themselves on the prairies and, after wandering around for several days, made their way to a farm-house, where they procured something to eat, though they were suspected of being rebels. They next, unfortunately, wandered into Alton, where, finding themselves objects of suspicion, they surrendered. Frank rejoined us only when on our way to be exchanged. The first tragedy under the regulation requiring the prisoners to go into the barracks or tents at dusk, occurred on the evening of May 2d. One of the prisoners was seated on the steps of his barrack washing his feet, when "retreat" sounded; a guard, standing almost beside him, ordered him in, but the man was a little slow in complying, as he had his feet in the water; the guard repeated the order twice, and then fired on the prisoner, inflicting a wound from which he died in about three weeks. The sentinel's conduct was approved, and he was promoted to be a corporal, but the precaution was taken not to place him on guard over the prisoners again, for fear of his meeting with an "accident."

On our arrival at Camp Butler the commander of the post was Col. Morrison, a superannuated officer of the regular army, kind hearted but very irascible. In his conduct towards the prisoners he was generally very lenient; soon after their arrival he had clothing and blankets issued to those who were insufficiently clad, and did them other favors. Towards his own men he was a martinet. On one occasion the colonel crossed the guard line and the sentinel failed to salute him; crossing a second time to make sure the sentinel saw him, he halted in front of the negligent guard, and in thundering voice demanded: "Do you know who I am, sir?" "Yes, sir," was the quavering response. "Why did you not salute me?" and without waiting for a reply, he seized the volunteer by the collar and administered to him a sound kicking. To the prisoners, accustomed to a perfect equality between officers and men, this was a novel sight and excited various comments. To the commissary officer of the post, a Virginian, and, it was said, a Southern sympathizer, the prisoners were greatly indebted for full rations and the privilege of trading any surplus for luxuries and merchandise at very reasonable rates. He had the reputation of being "square" in all his dealings, and was consequently much liked.

On our arrival, and for sometime after, the mortality at Camp Butler was great; up to the 25th of May there had been 318 deaths, a rate equivalent to 56 out of every 100 per year. During the month of May Maj. Fundy, of the Twelfth Illinois Cavalry, was given supervision of the Camp, and, by stricter sanitary regulations, the death rate was diminished, there being but 162 deaths from May 25th to September 6th, a rate of about 22½ out of every 100 per year. If it be taken into consideration that several hundred prisoners had escaped, the percentage of deaths will be somewhat greater than stated. Up to September 6th, the date of exchange, 225 had escaped, leaving 2,613; the average time of imprisonment was nearly twenty-six weeks—that is 1800 men 200 days and 1000 men, 146 days; the total number of deaths was 480, or 18⅓ out of every 100 for the six months, or 36⅔ per 100 a year. In this connection it is but fair to state that the provision made for the sick was ample; a good assortment of medicines was kept in the hospital drugstore, which, after our arrival, was placed in the charge of Joseph Hurd, of Co. K, a competent druggist. Among the prisoners were several surgeons, and in addition to these, Dr. J. Cooper McKee, U. S. A., was surgeon of the post. While he was in charge he ordered large additional supplies of medicine, and a room was fitted up exclusively as a drug store. When he was relieved, the latter part of July, a Springfield physician was placed in charge. The nurses were volunteers from the prisoners, among them N. K. Adams and Wm. H. Fay, of Co. K; D. P. Smith was

Mr. Hurd's assistant.

To resume the company diary: On the Sunday following our arrival it set in to storm, and on Monday there was a heavy fall of snow, a novelty to many who witnessed it. Spring now rapidly advanced, and by May 1st the trees were beginning to leaf, the grass was green and violets were in bloom. On the 23d of April there was seen the curious phenomenon of four mock suns, the real sun being in the centre. There was a brilliant electrical display on May 30th; for nearly an hour the flashes of lightning were almost incessant, but a few seconds intervening, while at times, for several minutes together, the play of electrical light would be absolutely without intermission. Occasionally great nebulous balls of fire would roll up from the horizon to the zenith, then would follow flashes of chain and forked lightning, diverging to every point of the heavens. No rain accompanied the electrical storm, but during its entire continuance there could be heard the distant low roll of thunder.

May 3d the camp was shocked by a tragedy in one of the barracks occupied by Mississippians: one of the prisoners, in a quarrel with a companion, seized a billet of wood and struck a fatal blow. The murderer was taken to Springfield and put in jail, but was not brought to trial, and when the prisoners were exchanged he was sent with the others.

May 9th, Thomas G. Roe (private, Co. K) died of measles. This was the first death in our company, and caused sincere sorrow. On the following day he was buried in the prisoners' graveyard, near the camp. Col. Morrison kindly permitted the company to accompany the body to the grave. William H. Fay read a chapter in the Bible and made a prayer. The grave was marked with a headboard inscribed with the name, company and regiment of the deceased.

Early on the morning of May 14th, A. J. Merritt (sergeant, Co. K) died of measles. Both he and Mr. Roe were sick from the time of our arrival. Mr. Merritt refused to give up, and remained in his tent till within a day or two of his death, when he became so weak as to be forced to go to the hospital. He was much depressed from leaving home and family, but both he and Mr. Roe died very peacefully.

On the morning of July 7th, John N. Cook (private, Co. K) died, and was buried the same day, the company receiving permission to attend. This was the last death in Co. K at Camp Butler.

On the 22d of June, Col. Fundy succeeded Col. Morrison as commander of the post. He was much less of a martinet, and was also popular with the prisoners in consequence of his showing them some favors. Occasionally through the summer he allowed the prisoners—several hundred at a time—to go to the river to bathe, under guard and an implied parole not to escape. The prisoners never, to the writer's knowledge, abused his confidence. He would listen to complaints, and, if well founded, would remedy the evil. At one time the militia—or, more properly, the recruits in an adjoining camp of instruction—made a practice of firing their muskets, loaded with ball, in such a direction that the balls fell in the prison enclosure. The whizzing of lead became a sound of daily occurrence, but the prisoners stood it very patiently till one of their number was struck and seriously wounded. A committee was then sent to Col. Fundy, to remonstrate and to plainly intimate that if the nuisance was not abated, the prisoners would themselves go out and stop it. He gave them patient audience, and promised them there should be no more trouble. About the middle of July he attempted an exercise of authority that cost him much of his popularity. For some time it had been customary to make details of the prisoners to do work outside the camp, they not being averse, as it gave them a slight relief from the monotony of prison life. On the 14th of July a detail was made as usual, but when they found that the duty was to bring in a Federal flagstaff and assist in raising it, they promptly refused to work. An attempt was made at coercion, but Col. Fundy, seeing that they would rather be shot down than obey, sent them back to quarters. Finding that none of the prisoners would volunteer, as a punishment, he cut down their rations, which, prior to this time, had been according to army regulations. Nothing more was done in regard to the flagstaff for a week, when a detail of Federal soldiers brought in the spar, and on the 29th attempted to raise it in front of headquarters—a large crowd of prisoners watching the operation, and greeting with a yell each failure. Finally, the blue-coats accomplished the feat, and, their hands relieved, they gave vent to their wrath by hurling a volley of sticks and brickbats at the jeering "rebs." The latter were not slow to send the missiles flying back, and the Federals, finding that in this game they were getting worsted, started for their muskets. Of course the Confederates at once dispersed, but a battery of artillery was brought out, so as to rake the street, and the guards were in a state of chronic scare for a day or two. The feeling between the prisoners and guards was not very friendly, and the former delighted in keeping the latter in fear of an outbreak. When there was a prospect of stormy weather, the prisoners in the tents would listen for the tramp of the sentinel, and when he approached within earshot, they would discuss the question of an outbreak, intimating that there was a plot to escape on the first stormy night. On several occasions the ruse succeeded so well that the garrison was kept under arms in the rain nearly all night.

Practical jokes were common among the prisoners, and served to relieve the monotony of their durance. A jovial Irishman in Co. E, on one occasion, went to the quarters of Co. K, and informed a number of his acquaintances that his mess had a pot of soup that they did not want, and invited them to bring their cups down and get some. The guests, with tin-cups and spoons in hand, followed their host to his tent, to find that the soup-kettle had been accidentally upset and its contents spread over the ground. Watching their opportunity, the disappointed soup-eaters invited their joking Irish friend, as he passed by, to sit down to a plate of fritters. He accepted, only to get a mouthful of cotton covered with batter and browned in the frying-pan. Sometimes the jokes were of a rougher character, as when a member of Co. C, who had eaten a very hearty dinner, was given a drink of sherry, wine of ipecac, surreptitiously obtained from the hospital.

Of books and other reading-matter there was a dearth, and, as at other prisons, the men resorted to trinket-making as a pastime. Rings, breastpins, crosses and similar articles were turned off in great quantities, every barrack and every tent being a manufactory. Bone, vulcanized rubber, cocoanut-shell, mussel-shells, gold and silver were the materials; old case-knives made into saws, files, camp-made bow-drills, pocket-knives and sand-paper the tools. From the rations of beef was obtained the bone; mussel-shells were gathered in Sangamon River by the water-details, the scanty pocket-money furnished the gold and silver, while the files, sand-paper and rubber in the form of buttons and rulers were procured by trading rations with the commissary. The delicately-shaded pink and white shells answered admirably for mother-of-pearl for inlaying. No little taste and ingenuity were displayed in the making of these articles.

The reception of the mail was an occasion of daily excitement, and the post-master was surrounded by an eager crowd while the names of the lucky few were called. Correspondence was limited to one page to a letter, but the number of letters was limited only by the prisoner's ability to pay postage. But few letters came through from the South, and the bulk of the mail was for the Tennessee troops and those having friends in the North. On June 28th a letter dated Camp Douglas, Chicago, was received by Eli Sears from J. Hearndon, giving us the first intelligence of those of the company who were left at Island 10, sick. As previously mentioned, these—nine in number—were sent to Madison, Wis., where J. F. Smith died, May 15th, and C. J. Moncrief on June 6th. Subsequently, we learned that E. F. Brown died September 4th, at Camp Douglas, to which camp they were transferred in June. The treatment of the prisoners at these two camps was very different from that at Camp Butler. No privileges were allowed; the rations were insufficient to satisfy the cravings of hunger, and as they were served to the prisoners cooked, there was not the variety which tends to keep men in health.

About the middle of August the prisoners were enlivened by the hope of exchange, and on the 1st of September the work of making out the exchange-rolls began. N. K. Adams, of Co. K, assisted, and from him were obtained the following figures:—

| Prisoners arriving at Camp Butler, | | 2,838 |
|---|---|---|
| Deaths, | 480 | |
| Escaped, | 225 | |
| Took the oath of allegiance, | 270 | |
| Total casualties, | | 975 |
| Remaining for exchange, | | 1,863 |

*First Alabama Regiment.*

| Arriving at Camp Butler, | | 326 |
|---|---|---|
| Deaths, | 30 | |
| Escaped, | 27 | |
| Total casualties, | | 57 |
| Remaining for exchange, | | 269 |

On September 2d, those who took the oath of allegiance—mostly from Tennessee—left for their homes. On the 6th, one-half of those to be exchanged took the cars for Alton, there to embark for Vicksburg; and on the following day the remainder started, excepting a few sick. The First Alabama prisoners were among the second detachment. Many of the cars were open platforms, and the trip in the hot sun to Alton was quite trying to those who had been so long imprisoned. At Alton the prisoners were transferred to transports, which left on the 8th and arrived at Cairo on the 9th. There the remainder of the Fort Donelson and Island 10 prisoners joined us, and, on Thursday, September 11th, the fleet steamed down the river. Several gunboats accompanied the fleet, which proceeded only during the day, anchoring or tying up to the bank at night. On the 12th, the fleet passed Island No. 10, whose deserted earthworks were fast caving into the river. At Memphis the fleet remained two nights and a day. While there Jerry Stuart, of Co. C, First Alabama, died and was buried. There were some twenty-one or twenty-two deaths among the prisoners while on the way down the river; and nearly every night or morning there was one or more rude graves dug on the bank wherever the fleet was lying, and the uncoffined dead left behind. On the 18th we passed a fleet of transports returning from Vicksburg with Federal prisoners. Sunday morning, September 21st, the fleet anchored above Vicksburg, at the appointed place of exchange; and on Monday morning the prisoners were disembarked and marched across the bend to the ferry opposite Vicksburg, where they crossed over. The sick on the hospital boat were transferred to a flag-of-truce boat from Vicksburg. The citizens had prepared a bountiful barbecue, and did everything for the prisoners' comfort that their limited means permitted. Lieuts. Hall and Tuttle met Co. K at Vicksburg—Capt. Whitfield going on to Montgomery, Ala., on a brief leave of absence.

# CHAPTER IV.

Capt. Isbell and his Battalion—Arrival at Port Hudson—Battle of
Corinth—The Reunited Regiment—Port Hudson—Land Defences—Red River Supplies.


Upon its arrival at Vicksburg, the First Alabama Regiment was quartered in the public-school building, where they remained several days. The city, even then, bore marks of the havoc of war. Shot and shell had torn huge rents in the walls of the houses, and ploughed up or dug great holes in which could have been buried a horse and cart. On the bluffs, and along the water-front, were batteries of heavy artillery, and soldiers were everywhere. Such an air of desolation pervaded the city that it was a relief to be ordered away. Two days after our arrival, on September 24th, A. P. Brown died of disease contracted at Camp Douglas. W. A. Dennis, who also returned sick, was sent to the hospital at Lauderdale Springs, where he died October 10th. On Saturday, September 27th, the regiment took the cars for Jackson, and, arriving there about noon, marched four miles out of the city, and went into camp near the Sweet Water Church. Here it remained till Wednesday, October 1st, when orders were received to proceed to Port Hudson. The regiment went by rail to Tangipahoa, La., and thence marched 33½ miles to Clinton, arriving on the morning of October 4th. The rest of the journey (20 miles) was made via the Clinton and Port Hudson Railroad. This road was not first-class, either in road-bed or equipment—flat rails, on rotten stringers and ties, one locomotive, one passenger car and half a dozen platform and box cars. Only half of our regiment could be transported at one trip; and, as it was the rule to run off the track at certain points, night had fallen before the two trips were made. The regiment encamped on the bluff in the rear of Battery No. 1 (afterwards Battery 2), between the village and depot.

After the surrender of Island No. 10, those who escaped, and others absent on leave, were collected at Fort Pillow and organized into three companies, under the command of Capt. R. H. Isbell. In this battalion there were the following members of Co. K: Lieut. M. E. Pratt, O. S. Norman Cameron, Corp. W. L. Ellis, Privates E. L. Averheart, Josiah Durden, John Griffin, E. Hearn, G. Hearn, W. H. Hutchinson, Junius Robinson and G. H. Royals. The battalion was attached to Gen. Villipigue's brigade; and soon after its organization was ordered to Grenada, Miss., where it remained some ten days doing provost duty. Thence it was ordered to North Mississippi to meet a raid of the Federal cavalry, but the enemy retired before its arrival. The summer months were spent in camp at Abbeville and Cold Water.

Late in September, Gen. Villipigue's brigade, including Capt. Isbell's battalion, was ordered to join Gen. Van Dorn. The brigade arrived at Corinth, and was attached to Lovell's division, forming a part of the right of the army. The first day's fight (October 3d) resulted favorably to the Confederates. On the second day it was planned that Gen. Price should attack in force on the left, and that, while thus engaged, Lovell's division should press forward and attack vigorously on the right. The attack was unfortunately delayed by the failure of Gen. Herbert to advance till 8, A. M., giving Gen. Rosecrans time to bring up fresh troops. Price drove the enemy before him, and penetrated into the streets of the town. Here his thinned brigades were attacked by the fresh troops of the enemy, and driven in disorder back over the ground they had won. Lovell, in the meantime, was advancing in pursuance of his orders, but had not yet engaged the enemy, when he received orders to throw Villipigue's brigade rapidly to the centre to cover the retreat of Price's broken ranks. This was gallantly done; and if Capt. Isbell's men had no opportunity to win laurels in the battle, they won a glorious meed of praise as a portion of the rear-guard in covering the retreat. So well was the duty performed that Rosecrans did not attack, and Gen. Van Dorn retired in safety. The only serious molestation was a skirmish at the Hatchie Bridge. After the retreat of the army to Oxford, Gen. Villipigue's brigade was ordered to Port Hudson, where it arrived November 5th. There was great rejoicing in the reunited company and regiment.

Gen. Villipigue died soon after his arrival (Nov. 9th), of cholera morbus, and his remains were sent to Richmond for interment, Corp. Ellis, of Co. K, being one of the escort.

The regiment now numbered nearly 700 muskets, having lost about 150 men since leaving Pensacola. Capt. Isbell's battalion brought with it a brass band; and, as the regiment was by this time fairly well drilled, it made a good military appearance on parade. The citizens of Mobile had presented the regiment with a uniform on its return from prison. Its guns, though in good order, were of a nondescript character—rifles, Springfield muskets, altered flint-locks and flint-locks; Co. K, being last on the list, had to put up with flint-locks. All the guns were, however, provided with bayonets, which gave them a uniform appearance. The men were in excellent spirits and condition. On the arrival of the regiment in October Cos. A, B and G were assigned to batteries, and on December 31st Co. K was assigned to a battery to be constructed.

Capt. Whitfield, who received a furlough after his exchange, arrived at Port Hudson on November 8th; Lieut. Pratt, on November 17th; and Lieut. Hall, who was furloughed at Jackson, December 5th.

Port Hudson is in East Feliciana parish, La., on the east bank of the Mississippi River, 25 miles above Baton Rouge. Before the war it was a place of considerable activity; about 30,000 bales of cotton and 2,000 hogsheads of sugar were shipped there annually; there were twelve or fifteen stores, and a population of some three hundred. The bluff is very high—nearly 80 feet above low water. At the time of the arrival of the First Alabama, there were fourteen or fifteen guns mounted, varying in size from 24-pounder siege guns to 8-inch shell guns, and one 10-inch Columbiad. During the following winter and spring several batteries were constructed and additional guns mounted, so that at the beginning of the siege, in May, 1863, the batteries and guns were as follows:—

Battery No. 1 (signal battery)—Co. K, First Alabama, one 30-pounder Parrott, calibre 4$\frac{62}{100}$ inches, siege carriage; one 20-pounder rifle (brass), calibre 4$\frac{62}{100}$ inches, siege carriage.

Battery No. 2—Co. A, First Alabama, one 42-pounder, smooth-bore, barbette carriage; one rifle (old 24-pounder, smooth-bore rifled, but not strengthened), barbette carriage; one ditto, siege carriage.

Battery No. 3—Co. G, First Alabama, one smooth-bore, 42-pounder; one rifle, calibre 6 inches (old 32-pounder), both mounted on barbette carriages.

Battery No. 4—De Gournay's battalion, one 10-inch Columbiad and one 8-inch Columbiad, Columbiad carriages.

Battery No. 5—Co. B, First Alabama, one 10-inch Columbiad, Columbiad carriage; one 32-pounder, barbette carriage.

Battery No. 6—De Gournay's battalion, one rifle (old 32-pounder); one rifle (old 24-pounder).

Battery No. 7—Tennessee company attached to De Gournay's battalion, hot-shot battery, two 24-pounders.

Batteries Nos. 8 and 9—De Gournay's battalion, each one 24-pounder, siege carriages, water batteries.

Battery No. 10—De Gournay's battalion, one 8-inch shell-gun, barbette carriage, water battery.

Battery No. 11—Miles' legion, one 20-pounder Parrott, extreme right of the land defenses.

The batteries were nearly all provided with bomb-proof magazines, but with no protection for the men except the low parapet. From Battery No. 1 to 11 it was a little over one mile.

A system of land defenses had been planned, and work slowly progressed during the winter of 1862-3. The full plans of the engineers were never carried out, and at the commencement of the siege the works on the northern side had not been begun. As planned the defenses began at Battery No. 11 and extended in a semi-circular direction for a distance of over four miles, striking the river near the mouth of Sandy Creek, about one mile above Battery No. 1. The earthworks, where completed, consisted of a crémaillère line, broken by occasional lunettes and redans for artillery. Where the ground was open and favorable to assault, the ditch was from three to four feet deep and five or six feet wide. From the bottom of the ditch to the top of the parapet it was, in no case, more than seven or eight feet, except when increased by the natural features of the ground, as in front of Battery No. 11, where there was a deep ravine. In Northern publications, maps are given showing a very complete system of defenses, with inner and outer lines, but these, if planned, were not constructed—there being but a single line of works, except that during the siege inner lines were constructed across points mined by the enemy, as at the northeast angle and Battery No. 11.

During the autumn and winter of 1862-3 communication was open between Vicksburg and Port Hudson, and both places were supplied with provisions from the Red River country. Transports arrived quite regularly from Red River at Port Hudson, until interrupted by the blockade established by Farragut in March, 1863. Cattle were driven from Texas for the use of the garrison; great herds of long-horned oxen swimming the Mississippi, was a curious but not uncommon sight. The cattle arrived in very good condition, but as there was but poor pasturage at Port Hudson some became skeletonized before they were slaughtered.

The commissariat during the six months preceding the siege was generally good. Plentiful rations of corn meal, beef, sugar, molasses and salt were issued, and sometimes potatoes. Some extras could also be purchased in the surrounding country, while the river and cypress ponds furnished fish.

The cooking was done in camp, the messes detailing some of their own number or hiring negro cooks. Ladies from the neighborhood quite frequently visited camp and showed much interest in the culinary department. A motherly old lady, on one occasion, after watching the movements of one of Co. K's cooks for some time, told the amateur, who had felt somewhat complimented by the attention, that she thought it would improve his kettles if he would burn them out. It is needless to say that he took the first opportunity of getting rid of the surplus soot and grease on his cooking utensils by following the advice.

# CHAPTER V.

Incidents in the Winter of 1862-3—An Unexpected Salute—A Parrott
for Co. K—Whitfield's Legion—Farragut's Fleet—Running the
Batteries—The Midnight Battle—A Crippled Fleet—Burning of
the "Mississippi"—Comparative Losses—The Land Attack—Incidents in April, 1863—A Sabbath Morning at Troth's Landing—
Close Quarters—Skirmishing.

Col. Steadman at once began a strict system of discipline and drill. The following was the order of the day: Reveille at daybreak with roll-call, inspection
of arms and policing of camps; 6 A. M., drill in the school of the soldier; 7 A. M.,
breakfast; 8.30 A. M., guard mounting; 9 A. M., non-commissioned officers' drill;
10 A. M., drill in the school of the company; 12 M., dinner; 1 P. M., skirmish drill; 3
P. M., battalion drill; 5 P. M., dress parade; sunset, retreat; 9 P. M., taps. Companies
assigned to batteries drilled at the guns at the hours for the company drill. Strict
regimental guard was kept up, all the requirements of the army regulations being
enforced.

The first call to action was on Sunday, November 16th, 1862, when the Federal
fleet appeared at the head of Prophet's Island, below Port Hudson. The regiment
was ordered to strike tents and pack knapsacks; while the left wing, including Co.
K, was deployed along the bank as sharpshooters. In a short time the fleet retired
and the troops were ordered back to camp.

On the evening of December 13, 1862, Capt. Boone's company of Light Artillery, supported by Co's D and F of the First Alabama, crossed the river and after
dark moved down opposite the anchorage of the iron clad Essex and a wooden
vessel. The guns, consisting of two smooth-bore 6-pounders and one 12-pound
howitzer were planted behind the levee, and at daylight the next morning fire was
opened on the wooden vessel. The fire was so effective that the Essex had to steam
up and interpose her iron sides for the protection of her consort. Both vessels then
retired down the river. Although the Federal vessels kept up a heavy fire our loss
was but one man wounded.

During the early part of December the regiment was busy constructing barracks of willow logs, the roofs covered with cypress boards. Co. K built two cabins,
which were completed about the last of the month. They were 18 by 22 feet, with
a large fireplace at each end. The chimneys were built of sticks daubed with clay.
An open door way furnished entrance and light, while ventilation was secured by
leaving the upper cracks between the logs unchinked; bunks were built in tiers
along the walls, and the men were very comfortably quartered for the winter.

On December 31st Capt. Whitfield received the promise of a one gun battery—a 30-pound Parrott gun—on the condition that his company build the battery and magazine. The battery was laid off above the redan, then known as Battery No. 1, but separated from it by a deep ravine. Co. K worked alone on their battery till January 8th, when details were made from the infantry companies of the regiment to assist them. By the 18th of January the work was so nearly completed that the gun was brought up from Battery No. 11 and put into position. The magazine was not completed till the last of February, the powder being stored in it on March 2, 1863. The gun was christened the "Lady Whitfield."

On December 26th, Lieut. Tuttle and Corp. John Hearn left for Alabama to secure recruits for Co. K. They returned in February having secured 45, as follows:—

| | |
|---|---|
| Adams, Jesse, | Mobile Co. |
| Alexander, J. L., | Autauga Co. |
| Boggan, Jno., | Wilcox Co. |
| Boggan, T. M., | Wilcox Co. |
| Boone, — — | Autauga Co. |
| Byrd, J. H., | |
| Callens, R. H., | Butler Co. |
| Clark, — — | Mobile Co. |
| Deno, M., | |
| Douglass, Wm., | |
| Dubose, Wm., | Pike Co. |
| Durden, G. W., | Autauga Co. |
| Glenn, Simeon, | Autauga Co. |
| Golsan, P. G., | Autauga Co. |
| Gorman, John, | Mobile Co. |
| Haley, — — | |
| Hamilton, John, | |
| Hern, M., | |
| Hays, J., | |
| Jenkins, E., | Pike Co. |
| Kirkpatrick, V., | Butler Co. |
| Lamar, M. D., | Autauga Co. |
| Leysath, E., | Butler Co. |
| Lewis, J., | Montgomery Co. |
| Martin, G. F., | Autauga Co. |
| Merritt, — — | |
| Mills, — — | |

McCarty, J.,

McDonald, — —

Owens, J.,                          Autauga Co.

Scott, B. L.,                       Autauga Co.

Scott, C. H.,                       Autauga Co.

Shaver, J. H.,                      Conecuh Co.

Simpson, J. L.,                     Butler Co.

Shoals, J.,                         Montgomery Co.

Schein, J.,

Smyth, A. C.,                       Butler Co.

Smith, Henry,

Stuart, J. J.,                      Wilcox Co.

Tarleton, M.,                       Lowndes Co.

Tharp, J. P.,

Vaughn, Wm.,

White, A. J.,                       Autauga Co.

Wilson, T. A.,

Winslett, — —

In addition to these Henry Fralick, of Autauga Co., joined the company in September, 1862.

Second Lieut. Dixon S. Hall having resigned from ill health, Junior Second Lieut. Tuttle was promoted, and an election was held March 4, 1863, for Junior Second Lieutenant, resulting as follows: John Frank, Jr., 35; Norman Cameron, 20; N. K. Adams, 8; John Frank, Jr., was thereupon duly commissioned.

On March 12, 1863, Moses Tarleton, of Lowndes Co., one of the recruits, died, and was buried with military honors. This was the only one of the company, owing in other cases of death to lack of opportunity, to whom these honors were paid.

Company K, having a full complement of men, and having but one gun in its battery, was divided as to duty. One portion was drilled as heavy artillery, another portion as infantry, while Lieut. Tuttle with the remainder was detailed to act with a detachment of the regiment under command of Major Knox as river police. The company was jocularly known, in consequence of this division, as "Whitfield's Legion."

On the afternoon of March 13, 1863, several of Admiral Farragut's vessels appeared in sight below Port Hudson, anchoring near the head of Prophets Island, and when the fog lifted on the morning of the 14th, his whole fleet lay at anchor just out of range of our guns. There were eight magnificent war steamers, one iron clad and six mortar boats. The flag ship was the steam-frigate "Hartford," with an armament of 26 eight and nine-inch Paixhan guns. The "Richmond," a ship of the same class, was armed with 26 eight and nine-inch Columbiads; the side-wheel steam-frigate "Mississippi" had 19 eight-inch guns, 1 ten-inch, 1 twenty-pound Parrott and 2 howitzers in her tops; the "Monongahela," steam-sloop of war, carried 16 heavy guns; the gunboats "Kineo," "Albatross," "Sachem," and "Genesee" each carried 3 heavy Columbiads and 2 six-inch rifles. All of these but the "Mississippi" were screw propellers. In addition to the above vessels all of which, except the "Sachem," were to attempt to run the batteries, there was the iron clad "Essex" carrying 10 heavy guns and also six mortar-boats, each carrying 1 thirteen-inch mortar. These last were to cover the advance of the fleet by fiercely shelling the Confederate batteries. The mortar-boats were moored close under the river bank at the head of Prophets Island, and were protected from the Confederate batteries by the bluff which at that point curved almost at a right angle. The "Essex" was anchored in the stream opposite the mortar-boats, and the other vessels some distance lower down but in sight.

On the afternoon of the 14th, the fleet opened fire apparently to get the range of our batteries. About seventy-five shot and shell were thrown, but the batteries made no response. All the batteries were manned as night approached, while the infantry were at the fortifications on the land side, prepared to resist any attack by Gen. Banks' forces. Until 9.30 P. M. all was quiet, then a red light was displayed from the mast-head of the "Hartford," the signal for the fleet to prepare for action. As the vessels passed his station, about 11 P. M., Capt. Youngblood, of the Confederate signal corps, sent up a rocket and the sentinels on the batteries fired their muskets, conveying the alarm from the lower to the upper works. In a few minutes the eighteen guns in position along the bluff were ready for action. At the wharf lay two Red River transports unloading; on board all was confusion, the shrieks of the women, the shouts of the officers to their crews, the glare of light from the cabins and furnaces, contrasted strangely with the death-like stillness and darkness of the batteries on the bluff. Just as the transports steamed away from the wharf on their way to Thompson's Creek, up which they sought safety, Gen. Gardner came dashing up to Battery No. 1, and seeing the lights on these vessels and mistaking them for the gunboats called out to Capt. Whitfield, "Why don't you fire on those boats?" John Hearn, not recognizing the General, replied, "They are our transports, you infernal thief." The commandant, either not hearing or concluding that under some circumstances deafness was commendable, made no response.

So soon as the alarm was given, the Federal fleet began firing; the mortar-boats—the "Essex" and the "Sachem"—moored to the bank or lying at anchor, with guns trained during the preceding day, had quite accurate range; but the practice of the moving vessels was somewhat wild till they were at close quarters. Orders had been issued to permit the enemy to get well in range before opening fire, and it was not until the leading vessel was nearly opposite Battery No. 11 that the first gun was discharged from the bluff. Instantly flash after flash revealed the positions of the Confederate artillery. The "Hartford," with the "Albatross" lashed to her larboard side, was in the advance; the "Richmond" and "Genesee," the "Monongahela" and "Kineo" followed, and the "Mississippi" brought up the rear.

At Battery No. 1 the upward passage of the fleet could only be traced by the flashes of its guns. Huge bonfires had been built under the bluff to illuminate the river, but the smoke of the pine wood only served to render impenetrable the darkness of the night, and they were immediately extinguished. Later in the battle, the signal corps, on the other side of the river, fired an old building, and the flames from this in a measure revealed the position of the vessels as they passed between it and the batteries. So soon as the Confederates opened, the fire of the fleet, no longer directed at random, was redoubled, and the roar of its hundred heavy guns and mortars, added to that of the rapidly-served artillery of the garrison, was fearful. Howitzers in the tops of the steamers swept the bluffs and gave some annoyance to the gunners. Leaving the rest of the ships to follow as best they could, the "Hartford" and her consort moved steadily on past the fortifications, rounded the point, and, pouring a farewell broadside of grape and shrapnel into Batteries Nos. 1, 2, and 3, steamed out of range up the river.

The "Richmond" and "Genesee" followed close in the wake of the "Hartford" till opposite Batteries Nos. 4 and 5, when a rifle-shell piercing the steam-drum of the former disabled her, and another shot passing through the smoke-stack mortally wounded Lieut. Boyd Cummings, her commander. A dozen other wounds in hull and rigging attested the accurate gunnery of the Confederates. Turning, by aid of her consort, both steamers came close under the bluff, where, for a few minutes, they were protected, and some one on board yelled out, with an oath, "Now let us see you hit us!" A moment later, as they ran out into the channel, both were raked. A shell exploding in the ward-room of the "Genesee" set the vessel on fire, but the flames were speedily extinguished, and after running the gauntlet a second time, the crippled ships got back to their anchorage.

The "Monongahela" and "Kineo" met with but little better fortune. A 32-pound cannon-ball cut the tiller-ropes of the former, another shot demolished the bridge and seriously wounded Capt. McKinistry, her commander, while her decks were strewed with dead and wounded. About the time the tiller-ropes of the "Monongahela" were shot away, a 32-pound ball struck the rudder-post of the "Kineo." Both thus disabled, the "Monongahela" ran into the bank, and the hawsers which lashed the ships together parting, the "Kineo" shot ahead and also ran into the bank. Backing off, the "Kineo" dragged with her the "Monongahela"; but the propeller fouled in the parted hawser, and the two vessels drifted helplessly down the river, letting go their anchors when out of range.

The pilot of the steamship "Mississippi," confused by the smoke of the battle, ran that vessel ashore at the point directly opposite Batteries Nos. 3, 4 and 5. Her commander, Capt. Melancthon Smith, used every endeavor to get his vessel off, but in vain. In the meantime her guns poured forth an almost continuous sheet of flame. Deserted by all her consorts she received the concentrated fire of the batteries. A rifle shot, probably from Battery No. 1, knocked a howitzer from her maintop clear of the vessel into the water. One after another her heavy guns had been disabled, and thirty of her crew had fallen, when her commander gave the order to abandon her. The dead were left on the decks, four of the wounded were taken ashore, others leaped into the river; those who were unhurt got to shore some by swimming and others in the boats. Before all had left the doomed vessel flames burst forth, by whom set is a disputed question. Capt. Smith reported that he fired the vessel, while the men in the hot-shot battery as strenuously insisted that she was fired by them, another report stated that a shell exploded in some combustibles arranged on her deck for the purpose of firing her. Some of those who escaped to shore made their way down the river bank to the fleet, swimming the crevasses; 62, including two officers, were taken prisoners the next morning. The flames spread rapidly, soon enveloping the hull and shrouds. As the flames reached the larboard guns, they were discharged one after another towards the vessels which had gone up the river, while shells on her decks kept up a constant fusilade. From the time that efforts had been given up to get her off, there had been a constant shriek of escaping steam from her safety valve. Lightened by the flames she floated off the bar and drifted, a huge pyramid of fire, down the river illuminating its broad expanse till all was bright as day, and revealing the shattered vessels of the fleet as they hastily steamed out of the way of their dangerous consort. Long after she had passed around the bend the light of the flames reflected on the sky marked her progress. About 5 A. M., when at almost the identical spot where the Confederate ram "Arkansas" was blown up, the fire reached the magazine and the "Mississippi" existed only in story. The shock of the explosion was felt at Port Hudson, twenty miles distant.

The battle lasted from about 11 P. M. to 2 A. M. Co. K fired their one gun 32 times. Lieut. Pratt had immediate charge of the gun, Capt. Whitfield being also present. Sergeants Ellis and Royals were the gunners and Wm. H. Fay the ordnance sergeant. Lieut. Tuttle was on duty with the river patrol. The eighteen Confederate guns fired altogether about six hundred shot and shell. Of which, according to Federal reports, at least one hundred struck the attacking vessels, as the "Hartford" alone was struck over thirty times. The loss of the First Alabama was three men slightly wounded. One man was killed at the land fortifications, and one man wounded in one of the lower batteries. Not a gun was injured.

The enemy's losses may be summed up as follows: the "Mississippi," burned; the "Richmond," completely disabled and obliged to return to New Orleans for repairs; the "Genesee," slightly damaged by fire; the "Monongahela," bridge shot away and tiller ropes cut; the "Kineo," rudder disabled and rigging badly cut up. Casualties, "Hartford," 3 killed and 2 wounded; "Albatross," 3 killed and 2 wounded; "Richmond," 4 killed and 7 wounded; "Monongahela," 7 killed and 21 wounded; "Mississippi," 22 killed and 8 wounded; and 62 prisoners: total 39 killed, 40 wounded and 62 prisoners, including 2 commissioned officers. One of the latter, Midshipman Francis, was paroled in consideration of his gallant efforts to save the lives of some Confederate prisoners, who fell overboard from the flag of truce steamer "Frolic," at Baton Rouge, a few weeks before, while en route to be exchanged. The other prisoners were sent to Richmond. Federal accounts of the battle state that the fire of the batteries was so accurate as to threaten the destruction of every vessel exposed. The gunners of Battery No. 1 labored under a disadvantage, as the smoke settled in a dense bank in front of the battery, but there was reason to believe that their gun did good execution.

Gen. Banks with 25,000 men was to have attacked by land, while Farragut assailed the river defences. On the evening of the 13th the divisions of Gens. Grover and Emory left Baton Rouge and were followed the next morning by Gen. Augur's division. Gen. Banks establishing his headquarters at the crossing of the Springfield road, seven miles below Port Hudson. Friday afternoon the enemy's advance guard encountered the Confederate pickets and a sharp skirmish followed, in which several men were killed and wounded. The following day there was another skirmish in which the Federals were worsted, losing a number of officers, killed, wounded and prisoners. They made no further demonstration till Monday when Gen. Rust's brigade attacked their rear guard as they were retiring and drove them six miles. The main body made no offer of battle, and the rear guard burned the bridges to prevent further pursuit. Thus ingloriously ended this attempt to capture Port Hudson by a force many times that of the garrison.

The mortar fleet, "Essex," and one or two other vessels, remained until March 28th, shelling the batteries, camps and transports at the wharves nearly every day, without, however, coming within range of the Confederate guns. On the 18th, the enemy landed a force of infantry and artillery on the west bank and burned the residence of Capt. Hines, the lower batteries shelling the raiders that night.

The "Hartford" and "Albatross" having gone up to Grand Gulf leaving the Red River open, several transports with supplies came down. On the 21st, while these were unloading, just above Battery No. 1, the fleet opened fire forcing them to steam up Thompson's Creek. The rifle shells fell around our battery and camp. On the 24th, the enemy fired a sugar-mill opposite Port Hudson, our batteries shelling them as they retired. A battery of light artillery planted by the enemy behind the levee shelled our lower batteries on the 25th but without effect. On the 28th the fleet steamed down the river. Admiral Farragut with the "Hartford," "Albatross" and ram "Switzerland," the last named having run the Vicksburg batteries, appeared above Port Hudson on April 6th, and on the 7th several vessels came up from below and exercised their guns for a while. There was a false alarm on the night of April 9th, caused by a raft with a fire on it floating down the river; it was boarded by the river patrol and the fire extinguished.

Rev. Mr. Baldwin, who had been appointed Chaplain of the regiment, preached his first sermon on Sunday, April 12th. Nothing of special interest beyond an occasional visit from the gunboats occurred until May 5th, when the fleet above Port Hudson fired the "Hermitage" and another building. On May 6th Co. K received another gun, a rifled brass piece, $4^{62}/_{100}$ inches calibre, captured on Amité river. It was clumsily mounted on a 24-pounder siege carriage, and christened "The Baby." In anticipation of receiving this gun a battery had already been prepared for it beside the old one.

The mortar fleet, the "Essex" and the "Richmond," having appeared again below Port Hudson, orders were received on May 9th for a detachment of Co. K to take "The Baby" to Troth's landing and at daylight on the 10th open fire on the fleet. The entire expedition under command of Lieut. Col. DeGournay consisted of one 24-pounder rifled, with a detachment from DeGournay's battalion; one $4^{62}/_{100}$ inch brass rifle, detachments from Co. K, First Alabama Regiment; one 20-pounder and one 12-pounder Parrott guns, with detachments from Miles' Legion. Of Co.

K there were 17 men, Sergeants Ellis and Royals, gunners, under command of Lieut. Tuttle. Soon after dark on the evening of the 9th a fatigue party began work, and during the night constructed a rude redoubt 12 by 24 feet, sinking it eighteen inches in the ground and throwing the earth to the front, thus forming an open earthwork with a parapet just high enough for the muzzles of the guns to project over. In this were placed the two larger guns, while the two Parrotts were placed in an old battery a few hundred yards lower down. From 11 P. M. till 1 A. M. the mortars shelled the batteries, but did not discover the working party. Shortly after 4 A. M. the earthwork was completed and the guns were put in position. While the fatigue party were still standing around, the flash and roar of the mortars caused a stampede of the non-combatants. As before, the shells were thrown at the batteries above, showing that the expedition was still undiscovered. The guns were loaded and so soon as it was sufficiently light were aimed at the "Essex;" then the command rang out "Fire!" The percussion shell from "The Baby" striking on the projecting point of land between us and the "Essex" exploded, the fragments rattling on the iron sides of that vessel. The guns were now loaded and fired as rapidly as possible, being directed at the "Essex" and mortar-boats. The latter were, however, moored close under the bluff and were secure except from fragments of bursting shells. As we afterwards learned the surprise of the enemy was complete; it took them but a few minutes, however, to recover, and shells from the mortars soon transcribed a shorter curve, exploding over our guns or burying themselves in the earth around them. Next the eight and nine-inch guns of the "Essex" opened, and a few minutes later a 100-pound rifle missile from the "Richmond" burst just as it passed the battery. The earth fairly shook as mortars, Columbiads, rifles and bursting shells joined in one continuous roar on that pleasant Sabbath morning. At the twenty-eighth shot, owing to the breaking of a chin-bolt holding on the trunnion-cap, "The Baby" was disabled. A few minutes before this the "Richmond" moved from her anchorage, and steamed towards the batteries; the last shot from the brass gun went hurtling through her rigging, and the last shot left in the locker of the 24-pounder struck her under the quarter; the Parrotts, from lack of ammunition, or some other cause, had ceased firing, so the batteries were silent. The "Richmond" came steadily on until within about 400 yards firing rapidly, then turning and giving in succession both broadsides she steamed back to her anchorage. The fleet now ceased firing and a death-like stillness followed the terrific roar of the battle.

Co. K had one man, Clark, wounded, a fragment of a shell cutting off two of his fingers. One man was mortally wounded and a Lieutenant severely wounded at the Parrott guns. There was also one or two casualties in the infantry support, and a man was killed in one of the regular batteries. The damage to the enemy was trifling; the "Essex" was struck about a dozen times by fragments of shell and once fairly by a solid shot. Four shot hit or passed through the rigging of the "Richmond." One of the mortar-boats was struck in the bow and another on the deck by fragments of shells, and it was reported that several of the crews were wounded.

As soon as the firing ceased ropes were attached to the trails of the guns, and they were drawn out of battery, limbered up and taken back to camp. The enemy, curiously, did not re-open fire during the removal, thus showing that they were very willing to have the guns taken away. When the "Richmond" was seen to leave her anchorage, Lieut. Pratt with the 30-pounder Parrott started for Battery No. 11, but before he could get there the steamer was out of range.

On May 12th and 14th the infantry companies of the regiment were sent to the breastworks in anticipation of an attack, a body of the enemy having cut the railroad between Port Hudson and Clinton. On the 14th there was a skirmish at Plain's store, six and a half miles from Port Hudson. Communication with Clinton was reopened on the 15th, and the accumulated mails of several weeks arrived, some 1,500 pounds of letters, greatly rejoicing the whole garrison. On Saturday, the 16th, there was another alarm, and a detachment of Co. K, with the brass rifle, was sent to the breastworks, remaining till Monday night, when they returned to camp. On the 18th a cavalry force under Col. Grierson made a raid on a small Confederate detachment guarding cattle, capturing the beeves and about 40 men. The same day four or five officers and privates of the First Alabama, who were fishing west of the river were captured. It was reported that Simpson of Co. K was among those picked up, but he came in the next day. On the 19th the infantry companies of the First Alabama were sent across the river and had a skirmish. Several of the enemy were killed, but our regiment suffered no loss. There was also skirmishing in the direction of Plain's store on the 19th and 20th. The fleet below had for some days been regularly shelling the batteries but without effect. On the 17th the "Genesee" came up within range of Battery No. 11 and was fired upon with a 20-pound Parrott. An Admiral's salute of seventeen guns was fired at noon on the 18th by the "Richmond," announcing, it was supposed, the return of Admiral Farragut. This brings us to the memorable siege of Port Hudson.

# CHAPTER VI.



The initiatory steps of the siege of Port Hudson may be reckoned from May 20th, 1863, when Gen. Augur, with his own and Gen. Sherman's division, advanced from Baton Rouge. Gen. Banks, who had been campaigning in the Teche country, embarking his troops at Shreveport, landed at Bayou Sara, five miles above Port Hudson, on the 21st. His forces consisted of the divisions of Gens. Grover and Emory, Gen. Weitzel's brigade of sappers and miners and two regiments of negro troops. A junction was effected with Gen. Augur's command on the 22d, thus closely investing the position. Gen. Banks then assumed command, his forces consisting of four divisions, one brigade and two unattached regiments, numbering from twenty-five to thirty thousand men. To resist this army, Gen. Frank Gardner had Beale's brigade, consisting of the First and Twenty-ninth Mississippi regiments, the Tenth and Fifteenth Arkansas and the Forty-ninth Alabama; Lieut.-Col. Miles' Legion; the First Alabama acting as heavy artillery; DeGournay's battalion of heavy artillery; a Tennessee company of heavy artillery; several companies of Mississippi light artillery, and some dismounted cavalry—all told, about six thousand men. Col. DeGournay, in an account of the siege, also mentions the Twelfth, Sixteenth, Eighteenth and Twenty-third Arkansas regiment, First Arkansas battalion, Ninth Louisiana battalion, a battalion of Texans from Maxey's brigade; but he places the number fit for duty at the beginning of the siege at only five thousand, the Arkansas regiments being skeletons.

On the 21st, Gen. Gardner sent out Col. Miles, with 400 cavalry and a battery, to reconnoitre in the direction of Plain's Stores. About four miles from Port Hudson they encountered Gen. Augur's advance, and a severe skirmish of two and a half hours followed. The Confederate loss was thirty killed and forty wounded. At the same time Col. Powers' cavalry, 300 strong, had a skirmish on the Bayou Sara road, and, being cut off, did not return to Port Hudson. When night fell the other forces were recalled within the fortifications. From Saturday, the 23d, to Tuesday, the 26th, the enemy were engaged in taking positions, the close investment being completed on the 24th. The First Alabama, with the exception of detachments at the guns, went to the front on the 23d, and were stationed on the northern line, at that time unfortified. Col. Steadman having been assigned to the command of the left wing of the garrison, Lieut.-Col. Locke commanded the regiment. Gen. Beale had command of the centre, and Col. Miles of the right. On the 24th there was heavy skirmishing, the First Alabama being engaged. The same day an order was issued for the brass rifle to be taken to a redan near the Jackson road. Lieut. Frank, with a detachment of the sick and cooks—the only men of the company in camp—went with the gun and opened fire at long range upon a battery of the enemy, which was soon silenced. This gun remained at the Jackson road redan during the entire siege, the gunners suffering severely, and the gun being several times dismounted. On the 25th the First Alabama was again heavily engaged skir-mishing, keeping back the enemy, while at the same time hurriedly fortifying, and lost twelve or fifteen men in killed and wounded. On the 26th the 30-pound Parrott was sent down to Battery No. 11 with a detachment of Co. K, under command of Lieut. Pratt, Sergt. Williamson, gunner, and a 24-pounder, rifled, was transferred from Battery No. 2 to No. 1. Lieut. Tuttle was in charge of Battery No. 1, and Lieut. Frank remained at the Jackson redan with the brass gun. Most of the 24-pounders were transferred from the river batteries to the fortifications, their places being supplied with Quaker guns. On the 26th there was but little firing, both armies preparing for the work of the following day.

Early on the morning of the 27th the enemy opened a heavy fire from both the land batteries and the fleet, and at 6, A. M., the Federal troops advanced to the assault. The heaviest attack was directed against the Confederate left, the assault-ing column consisting of Grover's and Emory's divisions, Weitzel's brigade and the two regiments of negro troops. On the extreme left the negroes, supported by a brigade of whites, crossed Sandy Creek and assaulted the position held by Col. Shelby with the Twenty-ninth Mississippi. They advanced at a double-quick till within about 150 yards of the works, when the 24-pounder in Battery No. 1, manned by Co. K, and two pieces of light artillery on Col. Shelby's line, opened on them; at the same time they were received with volleys of musketry from the Mis-sissippians. The negroes turned and fled, without firing a shot. About 250 of them were killed and wounded in front of the works; but the Federal reports stated that 600 were killed and wounded. If this were correct, they must have been shot down by the white brigade in their rear; and, indeed, volleys of musketry were heard in the direction of their flight. The First Alabama, Lieut.-Col. Locke, and the Tenth Arkansas, Col, Witt, engaged the enemy outside the entrenchments in the thick woods, and fought most gallantly; but were compelled, by the heavy force brought against them, to fall back across Sandy Creek. Col. Johnson, with the Fifteenth Ar-kansas, 300 men, occupied and fortified a hill jutting out from the line, and held it till the close of the siege, though desperate efforts were made to dislodge them; on the 27th they repulsed a very heavy assault, the enemy's dead in front of the position numbering eighty or ninety. Gen. Beale's command in the centre, and Col. Miles' on the right, were assailed by Augur's and Sherman's divisions about 2, P. M., but the enemy was everywhere repulsed with heavy loss. At the Jack-son road the detachment of Co. K, Lieut. Frank commanding, who were serving the brass rifle, were, with but one exception, killed or wounded. While ramming a charge home, Private Henry Smith was mortally wounded by a sharpshooter; Corp. Fergerson promptly stepped to his place, and was instantly fatally shot. In the meantime Private Hayes had been stricken down. Private Sears was busy attending the wounded and Lieut. Frank and Sergt. Ellis fired the gun themselves several rounds, the former pointing and the latter loading. While doing this Lieut. Frank fell, pierced by a Minie ball; by his request, Sergt. Ellis carried him out of the battery to Gen. Beale's headquarters, and gave him some water from the General's canteen. Sergt. Ellis then asked for more men, and the General sent his courier to the rear for a detachment, which came under Lieut. Tuttle's command. Lieut. Frank and Corp. Fergerson died that night; Private Smith lingered until July 10th; Private Hayes' wound was slight. Near the camp, Private Winslett was instantly killed by a shell while on his way to Battery No. 11 with the Parrott gun. The final effort of the day was made about 3, P. M., when the enemy, under cover of a white flag, made a dash on a portion of our lines, but they were easily repulsed. All day the fleet kept up an incessant firing upon the lower batteries, but did no damage. The Confederates had about 5,500 muskets at the breastworks; and had the men been evenly distributed, they would have been about three feet apart. Fortunately, the nature of the ground enabled Gen. Gardner to leave long stretches of the works defended only by pickets; and, as the charges were not simultaneous, troops were hurried from one point to another where most needed. The fortifications, as previously stated, consisted of an ordinary field earthwork, over any portion of which, at the beginning of the siege—it was materially strengthened during the 48 days at exposed points—a fox hunter could have leaped. In some places, in fact, as in front of the First Alabama, there were no breastworks. Against this small force and weak defences Banks hurled nearly his whole army of 25,000 men, who fought bravely, but were badly handled. Gen. Banks loss was 293 killed and 1,549 wounded; the Confederate loss was about 200 killed and wounded. The Confederates picked up outside the works the following night a considerable number of Enfield rifles. These guns, with others subsequently captured, were retained at the works, and ere the close of the siege most of the men were armed with two guns each—a musket loaded with buck and ball for use at close quarters, and a rifle for sharp shooting. As the fixed ammunition for the Enfield's became exhausted, the men used the powder from musket cartridges, and for lead picked up Minie balls fired into the place by the enemy. These Yankee leaden missiles were also used instead of canister and were so thick on the surface of the ground within our lines, that it was but the work of a few minutes to pick up enough to charge a 12-pounder gun.

During the bombardment, on the 27th, a rifle shell from the fleet struck in Battery No. 5 disabling the 10-inch Columbiad carriage and killing a private of Co. G, First Alabama. A squad from Co. K worked in that battery on the nights of the 27th and 28th in dismounting and remounting, after the repair of the carriage, this 10-inch gun, which was ready for service again on the 29th. The man who was killed was standing on the carriage and was literally torn to pieces.

On the 28th there was a cessation of hostilities at the breastworks for the purpose of burying the dead. Gen. Banks did not deem it worth while to bury the colored troops who "fought nobly," and their bodies lay festering in the sun till the close of the siege, when the colored regiments gathered the bones of their unfortunate brothers-in-arms and buried them.

At 7 P. M. the truce ended and the enemy made a furious rush upon the position held by the First Alabama. The fighting lasted nearly an hour, but the enemy were gallantly repulsed. The armistice did not embrace the river batteries and fleet, and the firing from the latter was unusually heavy. As previously mentioned Lieut. Pratt had received orders to take the 30-pounder Parrott, with a detachment from Co. K to Battery No. 11. An old 24-pounder, rifled, manned by a detachment from Col. DeGournay's battalion was also ordered to report to him at the same battery. His orders were to open upon the enemy's fleet at daylight, but owing to the darkness of the night and the road being torn up by shells, it was after sunrise when the guns were got into position. The battery was very small, having been built for one gun only, and the parapet was but little over knee-high. About 6 A. M., everything being in readiness, Lieut. Pratt opened fire with the two guns upon the "Essex" anchored one mile or more distant. Within ten minutes the little battery was receiving the concentrated fire of the fleet including the six mortar-boats. The "Essex," owing to her position, was the most accurate in her fire; three shells from her nine-inch guns exploded on the platform of the battery, and one struck a canteen hanging on the knob of the cascable of the Parrott. Private Joe Tunnell was slightly wounded by this shell; he was thrown upon his face and it was supposed he was killed, but he got up and brushing the dirt from his face exclaimed, "Well, boys they liked to have got me." His wound though not serious disabled him, and Lieut. Pratt, in addition to his own duties as commander, had to assist in serving the gun. Lieut. Pratt was himself wounded during the action, but did not leave the battery; he was standing on the parapet watching the effect of the fire, when a shell exploded in the earth under his feet, and threw him into the battery, while fragments of the shell struck him on the hand and hip. Never did men act with more coolness than those at these guns, nor has artillery often been more ably served. There were fired from Co. K's gun 49 shot and shell, and from the other piece 50. The enemy's vessels were struck repeatedly; one shell from the Parrott was seen to enter a port-hole of the "Essex," after which she closed her ports and, without firing another shot, retired out of range. The "Genesee" was also struck, and it was thought partially crippled. In addition to the casualties in Co. K, one man at the other gun was wounded.

The enemy made no more general assaults upon the works until June 14th, but in the meantime were approaching by parallels and planting batteries of heavy siege and naval guns. A steady fire was kept up day and night both by the fleet and the land batteries. There were about eighty siege pieces in these latter. An eight-inch howitzer so planted as to enfilade a portion of the southern line of defences, caused much amusement as well as annoyance to the Confederates. It was fired with light charges so as to make the shell ricochet and was, in consequence, christened "Bounding Bet" by the men, who speedily sought cover whenever they saw a puff of smoke from it. The deadly missile would go rolling and skipping along the inside of the line of works, finally exploding; one, that failed to burst, was opened and found to contain 480 copper balls of less than half an inch in diameter.

The sharp shooters were constantly engaged, and a man could scarcely show his head above the breastworks, at the more exposed points, without its being made a target. On May 31st the Parrott gun in Battery 11 fired a few rounds at the fleet. Soon after this Co. K was given a 24-pounder siege gun on the south side of the works named, by the company that had formerly used it, "Virginia," and the Parrott was transferred to DeGournay's battalion.

On the 3d of June an election was held in Co. K to fill the vacancy caused by the death of Lieut. Frank. N. K. Adams received 37 votes, W. L. Ellis 7, scattering 4, and Lieut. Adams was duly commissioned. Hot weather had now set in, and this, coupled with constant exposure in the trenches, caused much sickness among the troops; camp fever, diarrhœa, chills and fever soon reduced the number able to report for duty nearly one-third, and many of Co. K were among the sick. The company now served only at the artillery; Lieut. Pratt had charge of the "Virginia," on the south side of the fortifications, Lieut. Tuttle had "The Baby," brass rifle, at the Jackson Road, Lieut. Adams remained at Battery No. 1, occasionally relieving Lieuts. Pratt and Tuttle. Capt. Whitfield was placed in command of the Batteries 1, 2, 3 and 5, manned by detachments from Cos. K, A, G and B, respectively. The detachments of Co. K, at the "Virginia" and "Baby," were daily relieved by the men held in reserve at Battery No. 1. The fire of the enemy's land batteries was now very annoying, and the Confederate artillery could not fire a gun without having the fire of a dozen pieces concentrated upon it. Co. K's brass gun was in this way several times silenced, and during the siege had two or three sets of wheels cut down. Finally the artillerists were compelled to withdraw their guns from the batteries and only run them in when a charge was made. In a measure to meet this emergency, the ten-inch Columbiad in Battery No. 4, on the river, was turned around and brought to bear by calculation on the batteries giving the most annoyance, and fire opened, apparently with considerable effect as the enemy's fire slackened. Quite a number of eight and nine-inch guns were landed from the fleet, and placed in positions where they did much damage to the Confederate works. A battery of seven of these guns were located in front of Gen. Beale's centre, one of six guns to the right of the Jackson Road, in front of Co. K's brass gun, and one of seven guns in front of Col. Steadman's command. From all of these a constant fire was kept up.

A singular phenomenon occurred on the night of June 13th; after a heavy cannonading an immense wave, at least six feet in height, rushed up the river, and at the same time Battery No. 6 caved into the river, one gun being lost. Whether the wave caused the bluff to cave in, or the bluff caving caused the wave, was a disputed question in camp, the general opinion, however, was that not a sufficient mass of earth fell to cause such a disturbance of the river.

About 3 A. M. on the 11th, after a heavy bombardment, the enemy made an attempt to storm the southeast angle of the works, but were repulsed. On the morning of the 13th a tremendous bombardment was opened, and a show of force was made. The firing then ceased and Gen. Banks sent in a flag of truce, demanding the surrender of the place. He complimented the garrison and commander in high terms; their courage, he said, amounted almost to heroism, but it was folly for them to attempt to hold the place any longer, as it was at his will, and he demanded the surrender in the name of humanity, to prevent the sacrifice of lives, as it would be impossible to save the garrison from being put to the sword when the works should be carried by assault; his artillery was equal to any in extent and efficiency, and his men outnumbered the garrison five to one. Gen. Gardner simply replied that his duty required him to defend the post.

Before day on the morning of June 14th the enemy's land batteries and the fleet opened fire with unusual rapidity, and about daylight the assault began. From the northeast angle to the Jackson Road the fighting was the most severe; the line between these points was defended by the First Mississippi and Forty-ninth Alabama and three or four pieces of artillery, including Co. K's brass rifle at the Jackson Road. Gen. Banks' plan of attack was as follows: two regiments of sharp shooters were ordered to advance as skirmishers, these were followed by a regiment with hand grenades, while another rolled up cotton bales to fill the ditch. Weitzel's brigade and two brigades commanded by Cols. Kimball and Morgan, all under command of Gen. Weitzel, formed the storming party. On the left of this command was Gen. Emory's division under command of Gen. Paine.

The Federals advanced, through their parallels, to within three hundred yards, and then, under cover of the dusk of the early morning and the smoke of their artillery, formed their line of battle, and advanced to the assault, in many places approaching to within ten feet of the works. They were received, however, with so deadly a fire of "buck and ball" that they were everywhere driven back with heavy loss, or crouched in the ditch for protection. By mere physical pressure of numbers some got within the works, in front of the First Mississippi and Forty-ninth Alabama regiments, but were instantly shot down. Co. K's brass rifle did good execution; Lieut. Tuttle was in command and Sergt. Royals was gunner. In the midst of a terrific shower of rifle balls, it was served with coolness and deliberation. The enemy's hand grenade experiment proved an unfortunate one for the assailants, as very few exploded when thrown in—they were percussion grenades—but when thrown back by the Confederates, from the slightly elevated works, into the midst of the Federals below, they exploded, carrying death to their former owners. The fight lasted, with great severity, for about two hours, when the infantry fell back, but a heavy artillery fire was kept up all day. About one hundred prisoners were captured in the ditch near the Jackson Road, being unable to retreat. Among the Federal troops, who especially distinguished themselves here, were the Eighth New Hampshire and Thirty-eighth Massachusetts regiments. The fighting was very severe in front of the First Alabama, but the enemy did not get so near the works. On the right a feint was made, but the enemy did not approach to within close musketry range. In front of the 24-pounder, "Virginia," manned by Co. K, they approached near enough for shrapnel, and Lieut. Pratt sent a few shell into their ranks, but they soon withdrew. The enemy's official report of the losses, was 203 killed, 1,401 wounded, 201 missing, total 1,805. Probably many of those reported missing were killed, as there were 260 Federal dead buried in front of the centre alone, while the number of prisoners taken was but about 100.

After this repulse, Gen. Banks sent no flag of truce for the purpose of burying the dead or removing the wounded for three days. On the 17th Gen. Gardner sent out a flag and requested the Federal commander to bury his dead; but he replied that there were no dead to bury. Gen. Beale, at Gen. Gardner's request, then sent a flag to Gen. Augur, who commanded in his front, calling his attention to the unburied dead. Gen. Augur replied that he did not think there were any there, but would grant a cessation of hostilities to see. Parties of Confederates were detailed to collect and pass over to the Federals the dead near our lines, and, as above stated, 260 were thus removed. Among the dead was found a wounded officer—a Captain—who had been lying exposed to the sun for three days without water, and was fly blown from head to foot. At the close of the siege the writer was informed that this man recovered. During the three days many wounded must have perished on the field, as they could be heard crying piteously for help. A Confederate, more tender-hearted than Banks, was shot by the enemy while carrying a canteen of water to a wounded Federal who lay near the works. In front of Col. Steadman's position the dead were not buried, and their bodies could seen from the breastworks, at the time of the surrender, twenty-five days after the fight.

On June 15th Co. K removed a 42-pounder, smooth-bore, barbette carriage, from Battery 2 or 3 to Battery No. 1, to replace the 24-pounder siege piece which had been sent to the land defences.

During the remainder of the month, there was an incessant fire of sharp shooters and artillery. To the left of the Jackson Road, the enemy built up a tower of casks filled with earth, two or three tiers in height, from which their sharpshooters were able to over look the Confederate works, and keep up an annoying fire. It was not more than 60 yards from our lines, but the two or three pieces of artillery which could be brought to bear on it, were commanded by a score of the enemy's heavy guns, and could not be used to batter it down. At other portions of the line the enemy rolled bales of cotton to within close range, and surmounted them with sand-bags, arranged with narrow loop-holes, for the sharpshooters. On the 25th, Corp. L. H. Skelton, of Co. F, First Mississippi regiment, crawled out and placed port-fires in the bales of cotton and fired them; the first attempt failing, he went out a second time and succeeded in burning a number of bales. On the night of the 26th, 30 men made a sortie near the southeast angle, spiked the guns of one of the enemy's batteries, and captured seven prisoners.

Co. K began about the last of June to make an excavation, partially behind the Jackson Road redoubt, in which to place their brass rifle, with a view of battering down the sharp shooters' tower. It was intended to be so constructed as to be protected from the enemy's artillery, but as the work could only be done at night, it was not completed in time to be of essential service. J. McCarty was killed at the brass gun, on June 23d, by a fragment of a shell. This was the last casualty in the company during the siege.

While these events were in progress in the centre, the enemy had been busy, on the extreme right, preparing to assault Battery No. 11, which was the key to the Confederate works. They erected a battery containing 17 eight and nine-inch smooth bore guns and 20-pounder Parrotts, on the opposite side of the ravine and distant only 150 yards. On the opposite bank of the river, Parrott guns, manned by

United States Regulars, were planted. Lieut. Schurmer, of DeGournay's battalion, was in command of Battery 11, and its defense could have been entrusted to no more gallant gentleman. Gen. D. H. Hill, in a letter to the writer, said, "I knew Schurmer well at Yorktown," and in a subsequent number of his magazine related the following incident connected with the siege of that place, where Schurmer was under his command: Schurmer was in charge of a 42-pounder, and especially distinguished himself by the accuracy of his fire. It was regarded as remarkable, even in the Federal army, and one of the French princes, on McClellan's staff, made mention of it in a report of the operations at Yorktown. When Yorktown was evacuated he remained in Fort Magruder firing the 42-pounder all night, thus contributing essentially to the deception of the enemy. He attempted to escape the next morning on foot, but, exhausted, fell asleep by the wayside and was captured.

In Battery No. 11 was the 30-pounder Parrott formerly in Battery No. 1. On Friday morning, June 26th, the fleet and land batteries opened a terrific fire on the earthwork, and in a few minutes Co. K's old gun was forever silenced. One shell exploded in the muzzle, breaking off about a foot of it, while the carriage was struck by five or six shots and cut down. Three times during the day the Confederate flag was shot away, falling outside the works, and each time Schurmer, regardless of the storm of shot and shell, replaced it. Without intermission by day or night, the enemy kept up this fire until the 30th, and under cover of it advanced their parallels down through the ravine to within fifteen feet of the battery. Gallant Schurmer never relaxed his heroic devotion to duty, and on the 29th fell dead at his post. The next day while the Confederates were rolling ten-inch shells over the parapet into the enemy's ditches, a storming party of some two hundred men made a rush for the battery. Its squad of defenders were hastily reinforced and the assailants were driven out, leaving sixteen dead inside our lines. On July 4th the Federal sappers were driven out of their ditches by hand grenades, but they claimed, after the surrender, that they had mined Battery 11 and had 3,000 pounds of powder under it ready to explode had the siege been further prolonged. The enemy's batteries, on the west bank of the river, occasionally opened but were always silenced by Batteries 3, 4 and 5. On the centre of the south side the enemy kept quiet, and the detachment of Co. K, at the 24-pounder, had but little to do. A few shots were fired on the 2d of July.

At the northeast angle the enemy, during the latter part of June and the first of July, were very busy mining, but the Confederates were no less industrious. An inner line of works extending across the angle was thrown up, the enemy's mine was countermined, and on the 4th blown up. The enemy's sappers were also constantly annoyed by rolling ten-inch shells into their ditches. On July 4th the enemy fired salutes from all their batteries with shotted guns, making it a warm day within our lines.

On the night of the 6th, Co. K completed the sunken redoubt for the brass rifle, and on the following morning opened fire on the sharpshooters' castle; but the embrasure was incorrectly laid off, and the gun could not be brought to bear on the tower without firing so close to the side of the embrasure as to cause the earth to cave in; so that, after firing three shots, the gun could no longer be brought to bear on the mark. Owing to the fire of the sharpshooters, nothing could be done to correct the mistake till night. The necessary changes in the earthwork were made that night, and on the morning of the 8th the detachment was at the gun ready to open fire, when the flag of truce was raised.

The condition of the garrison was now such as to limit further resistance to a few days. Early in June the enemy's shells had fired the commissary building and mill, destroying several thousand bushels of grain and the chief means of grinding what was left. Fortunately, the only locomotive of the Clinton and Port Hudson Railroad was at Port Hudson. This was blocked up, and furnished power to drive a portable mill. The corn, with the exception of two or three days' rations, held in reserve for an emergency, failed the last of June, and the supply of meat failed about the same time. There still remained a considerable stock of field peas and mules. When the men of the First Alabama were asked if they would eat mule, they replied, "Yes; give us dog if necessary." The same spirit animated the whole garrison. Mules were slaughtered, and the meat issued on the 29th or 30th of June; the peas were issued whole and also ground into meal. Those sick in camp and hospital were fed by their comrades upon rats, daintily served up as squirrels. In the pea diet there were some drawbacks; the peas were stored in bulk on the floor of the church, and the concussion of the bombardment had broken in every pane of glass in the building. This, in comminuted form, was mingled with the peas; and it was no unusual incident to be made painfully aware of its presence in masticating the peas. There were some among the garrison who could not stomach the mule, and, to satisfy these, an unexpected discovery was made of sixty barrels of corn beef. Some wonder was expressed as to this windfall, but it was accepted, eaten in good faith and pronounced excellent. It was not until after the surrender that those who ate it knew that it was carefully corned mule.

The ammunition, although it had been economized, was so nearly fired away that another general assault would have exhausted the supply. Nearly every cannon on the land fortifications had been disabled, and in the river batteries there remained but nine or ten fit for use.

On the first day of the siege there were 5,500 men at the breastworks; some 600 had been killed and wounded; many had died of disease, and at least 2,000 were suffering from camp-fever and diarrhœa, many of them being unable, under any emergency, to fire a musket.

This was the situation when, on the 7th of July, salutes from the enemy's batteries and fleet, and continued cheering all along their lines, announced some great event. The lines were so close that the garrison was not long kept in ignorance that Vicksburg had fallen. That night Gen. Gardner summoned a council of war, consisting of Gen. Beale, Cols. Steadman, Miles, Lyle and Shelby, and Lieut.-Col. Marshal J. Smith. They decided unanimously that it was impossible to hold out longer, inasmuch as the provisions were nearly exhausted; of ammunition there remained but twenty rounds per man, with a small supply for the artillery; and a large proportion of the garrison were sick or, from exhaustion, unfit for duty. A communication was at once sent to Gen. Banks, stating what had been heard in regard to the fall of Vicksburg, asking for official information and notifying him that, if the report was true, Gen. Gardner was ready to negotiate for terms of surrender. Gen. Banks' reply, enclosing a despatch from Gen. Grant, announcing the fall of Vicksburg, was received before day. Gen. Gardner at once appointed Cols. Miles and Steadman and Lieut.-Col. Smith commissioners to arrange terms of surrender. To represent the Federals, Gen Banks appointed Brig.-Gen. Chas. P. Stone, Brig.-Gen. Wm. Dwight and Col. Henry M. Birge. The following terms were drawn up and signed:—

*Article I.*—Maj.-Gen. Frank Gardner surrenders to the United States forces, under Maj.-Gen. Banks, the place of Port Hudson and its dependencies, with its garrison, armaments, munitions, public funds and materials of war, in the condition, as nearly as may be, in which they were at the hour of the cessation of hostilities, namely, 6 o'clock, A. M., July 8, 1863.

*Article II.*—The surrender stipulated in Article I is qualified by no condition save that the officers and enlisted men comprising the garrison shall receive the treatment due to prisoners of war according to the usages of civilized warfare.

*Article III.*—All private property of officers and enlisted men shall be respected, and left to the respective owners.

*Article IV.*—The position of Port Hudson shall be occupied to-morrow at 7 o'clock, A. M., by the forces of the United States, and its garrison received as prisoners of war by such general officers of the United States service as may be designated by Gen. Banks with the ordinary formalities of rendition. The Confederate troops will be drawn up in line, officers in their positions, the right of the line resting on the edges of the prairie south of the railroad depot, the left extending in the direction of the village of Port Hudson. The arms and colors will be conveniently piled, and will be received by the officers of the United States.

*Article V.*—The sick and wounded of the garrison will be cared for by the authorities of the United States, assisted, if desired by either party, by the medical officers of the garrison.

CHAS. P. STONE, *Brig.-Gen. U. S. A.*

W. N. MILES, *Col. Com. Right Wing, C. S. A.*

WM. DWIGHT, *Brig.-Gen., U. S. A.*

I. G. W. STEADMAN, *Col. Com. Left Wing, C. S. A.*

MARSHAL J. SMITH, *Lt.-Col. & Chief of Art., C. S. A.*

HENRY W. BIRGE, *Col. Com. 5th Brig., Grovers Div., U. S. A.*

Approved,

N. P. BANKS, *Maj.-Gen.*

Approved,

FRANK GARDNER, *Maj.-Gen.*

On the morning of the 9th, the garrison was formed in line and two officers were sent, by Gen. Gardner, to conduct in the Federal officer deputed to receive the surrender. This was Gen. Andrews, who entered the lines on the Clinton Road shortly after 7 o'clock. Gen. Gardner met him at the right of the line and delivered up his sword, saying, "General, I will now formally surrender my command to you, and for that purpose will give the command "Ground arms." Gen. Andrews replied, that he received Gen. Gardner's sword, but returned it to him for having maintained his defence so gallantly. Meanwhile the Federal infantry moved in, and the wings resting on the river cut off any attempt to escape. A few officers and men, including Maj. Knox, of the First Alabama, concealed themselves near the outer lines, prior to the surrender, and the following night made their escape. There were, all told, 6,233 prisoners surrendered, but this included many non-effectives, such as teamsters, commissary, quartermaster and ordnance employees. At no time were there more than 5,500 muskets at the works. There were also surrendered 5,000 stand of firearms and 51 pieces of artillery, the latter including a number of small cast-iron guns, not mounted, and a number of disabled guns. The small number of muskets surrendered is accounted for by the fact that many of the soldiers threw their guns into the river or broke them.

The casualties in the First Alabama regiment during the siege were as follows:

| | | | | | | | | |
|---|---|---|---|---|---|---|---|---|
| Co. | A, | Killed, | 3, | Wounded, | 17, | Died of disease, | 4 |
| Co | B, | Killed, | 5, | Wounded, | 4, | Died of disease, | 1 |
| Co | C, | Killed, | 3, | Wounded, | 9, | Died of disease, | 1 |
| Co | D, | Killed, | 6, | Wounded, | 7, | Died of disease, | 2 |
| Co | E, | Killed, | 4, | Wounded, | 6, | Died of disease, | 2 |
| Co. | F, | Killed, | 12, | Wounded, | 6, | Died of disease, | |
| Co | G, | Killed, | 5, | Wounded, | 9, | Died of disease, | 1 |
| Co | H, | Killed, | 4, | Wounded, | 6, | Died of disease, | 1 |
| Co | I, | Killed, | 2, | Wounded, | | Died of disease, | |
| Co | K, | Killed, | 4, | Wounded, | [1]6, | Died of disease, | 4 |
| | Total, | | 48 | | 70 | | 16 |

Co. K's casualties were as follows: Lieut. Frank, Corp. Fergerson and Private Winslett killed May 27th; Private McCarty, killed June 23; Private Henry Smith, mortally wounded, May 27th, died July 10th; Lieut. Pratt and Private Josiah Tunnell, wounded May 28th; Private Clark, wounded May 10th, at Troth's Landing; Private Hayes, wounded May 27th and Sergt. Williamson, wounded during the siege. Private Boon, died June 29th, of disease, Private Scott, July 3d, Private Mills, July 5th, Private Holston, July 6th.

During the siege two or three private families remained in the town, but suffered no casualties excepting one accidental; a boy having found an unexploded shell was playing with it when it burst, seriously wounding himself and mother.

---

[1] One mortally.

# CHAPTER VII.

Experiences of Paroled Prisoners of War—A Disorganized Regiment—A Handsome Turnout—Close Quarters—A Faithful Servant—Present, or Accounted for—In Camp at Meridian.

During the negotiations for the surrender, Gen. Banks refused to grant terms permitting the release of the prisoners on parole, on the ground that orders from Washington positively forbade it. On the day of surrender, however, he suddenly changed his mind and decided to parole all enlisted men, retaining the officers. Gen. Dick Taylor's capture of Brashear City, and his nearly successful attack on Donaldsonville, threatening communication with New Orleans, may have had some influence in causing the change of purpose. Gen. Wirt Adams' audacious dash into Springfield Landing and his destruction of a large amount of commissary supplies stored there, seriously embarrassing the Federal commander in feeding his own troops, also made the paroling of the prisoners advisable. There is no doubt, however, that Gen. Banks was influenced by an honest admiration of the gallantry and fortitude of the garrison, and this was his avowed reason for paroling them. Blanks were at once printed, Private J. C. Rogers, of Co. K, acting as the printer, and on Saturday, July 11th, the giving of the paroles began.

The paroling of the First Alabama was completed Tuesday forenoon (the 14th), and in the afternoon the regiment, with the exception of those in the hospitals, bade farewell to their officers and marched out of the fortifications. Of Co. K, but one was left behind—James Herndon, who died a few days later. Altogether, about 500 enlisted men of the garrison were left behind in the hospitals, sick and wounded.

The regiment kept well together till they were fairly outside the enemy's lines, and then, in the absence of the commissioned officers, all organization was at an end. About eight miles from Port Hudson the main body of the regiment encamped, but some of the men marched on, and all through the night squads were leaving. No attempt was made in the morning to keep the men together. Maj. Knox, who escaped, and who joined the regiment after it was outside Gen. Banks' lines, rode forward to secure rations for the regiment, but failed, and we did not see him again till we reached Shubuta, where he made arrangements for our transportation to Mobile.

Most of Co. K, and of the First Alabama, took the direct road to Shubuta, a station on the Mobile and Ohio Railroad. At Clinton, Privates J. H. Byrd and A. J. White went to the hospital, where both died on July 25th.

The writer can only give the experiences of a party of eight, of which he was one, on the homeward trip, but all probably fared about alike. Our party consisted of Orderly Sergt. Cameron, Sergt. Fay, Corp. Blaylock, Privates Bledsoe, Hurd, Lamar and Smith and a youth named Dennis, who was with the company but not mustered in. On the second day after leaving Port Hudson, members of the squad purchased a horse, mule and Jersey wagon, with which to carry our baggage and sick. The wagon had well-worn wooden axles which constantly broke; the horse was sore back and skeletonized, but the mule was a very fair animal. With this team we left Clinton on the morning of the 16th, but just before night halted for repairs, having made fifteen miles. On Friday, the 17th, after the wagon had been overhauled at the wayside smithy, we marched to Tangipahoa, eighteen miles. Two of the party, with the wagon, left early the next morning for Summit, Miss., while the others remained at Clinton till Sunday afternoon, and then took the train on the N. O. & J. Railroad, arriving at Summit at 9, P. M. So soon as we got off the Confederate cavalry burned the train, to prevent it falling into the hands of the enemy. The wagon detail arrived just before the train, having broken down on the road, necessitating the making of two axles. On Monday morning we started due east for Monticello, and camped after marching twenty-two miles. At 11, A. M., Tuesday, we reached Monticello, where we found Gen. Logan's command (Confederate) crossing Pearl river. At Tangipahoa we drew rations, and at Monticello Gen. Logan's commissary honored Sergt. Cameron's requisition. From Monticello we took the Williamsburg road through the piney woods, scoring for the day twenty-one and one-half miles. Now began daily skirmishes for something to eat, as those who were ahead of us had cleaned the section adjoining the road like a cloud of locusts—there was little left to beg, buy or steal. On Wednesday we scored nineteen and one-half miles, dining, for a consideration, with a probate judge. A shower coming up, we stopped at dusk one mile west of Williamsburg at a log cabin—one room and a shed. The family consisted of a man, his wife, two sons and two daughters. The paroled soldiers who had been passing for two days had nearly drained them of everything, but they treated us very cordially, gave us supper and breakfast of corn-bread and bacon, and spread us a pallet of quilts across the floor in front of the fire. With difficulty could they be induced to accept even a trifling compensation. In addition to our party of eight, there were three other soldiers. The lady (poor and ignorant, she was a lady) occupied the shed room with her two daughters, while the host, his two sons and eleven guests slept in the main room. It was our experience all along the route that, while there was no cause of complaint against any, the poor were the more hospitable. Friday night our party went supperless to our blankets in a roadside camp.

Saturday afternoon we arrived at Shubuta, where we found collected a large number of the paroled prisoners awaiting transportation. It was about midnight when the train going south came along. As it was already full to overflowing, those at Shubuta had to climb to the second deck and take passage upon the roofs of the freight cars. It was a ticklish position, but we lay down, secured ourselves as best we could and went to sleep. At 9, A. M., Sunday, the train arrived at Mobile, and the smoke and dust begrimed deck passengers of Co. K wandered down to the river and performed ablutions in rain water collected in a lot of iron salt-boilers lying on the wharf. At 1, P. M., we took the train for Montgomery, whence the members of Co. K soon made their way home.

As illustrating the faithfulness of the negro, it is worthy of record that Lamar's colored boy Floyd, who was with him at Port Hudson, and who soon after the surrender was missing, was awaiting his master with a horse at Washington Landing. He had got into a fight with a Federal negro soldier, knocked him down and then fled, fearing that he would be conscripted into the Federal army, and had made his way home.

John Tarleton died on his way home, near Monticello. Seven men, Jesse Adams, M. Deno, — Haley, M. Hern, — Merritt, J. Schein and J. Shoals never afterwards reported to the company: Jesse Adams was known to have made his way to Mobile.

The other members of Co. K succeeded in getting to their homes, where they remained, enjoying a well earned furlough, until Oct. 12, 1863, when the First Alabama was ordered to report at Cahawba, Ala.

Of Co. K, according to such imperfect records as the writer has at his command, the following men reported at Cahawba, or soon after at Meridian, Miss.: Orderly Sergeant, Norman Cameron, J. L. Alexander, E. L. Averheart, O. M. Blaylock, J. Boggan, T. M. Boggan, G. R. Bledsoe, C. W. Brown, Wm. Douglass, Wm. Dubose, George M. Durden, J. Durden, W. L. Ellis, W. H. Fay, W. Farmer, Henry Fralick, P. G. Golsan, John Gorman, John Griffin, J. Hamilton, J. C. Hearn, G. W. Hearn, E. Hearn, Joseph Hurd, W. H. Hutchinson, E. Jenkins, J. Killough, V. Kirkpatrick, M. D. Lamar, E. Leysath, J. Lewis, G. F. Martin, J. W. May, Wm. Moncrief, J. Owens, James D. Rice, Junius Robinson, C. H. Royals, G. H, Royals, E. T. Sears, J. H. Shaver, J. L. Simpson, D. P. Smith, A. C. Smyth, A. J. Thompson. John S. Tunnell, Josiah Tunnell, Wm. Vaughn, John Williamson and T. A. Wilson. J. J. Stuart and J. P. Tharp reported not very long after, and R. H. Kirkpatrick was received as a recruit, total 53. There were absent at the hospitals or invalided: R. H. Callens, at Selma, and J. Hays, at Montgomery, both of whom soon after died; S. Glenn, J. C. Rogers, B. L. Scott and F. Wilkins, all of whom soon after received discharges for disability. Clark had been transferred to the navy during the summer.

The officers of Co. K, Capt. Whitfield and Lieuts. Pratt, Tuttle and Adams, were taken by boat to New Orleans, and quartered on Rampart street. Here they remained till Sept. 20th. They were then transferred to Johnson's Island, Lake Erie, where they arrived on Oct. 1, 1863. Lieut. Adams was exchanged in the spring of 1864, rejoining his company in May. Lieut. Pratt was paroled Sept. 16, 1864. Capt. Whitfield and Lieut. Tuttle remained at Johnson's Island till the close of the war.

Of the regiment 610 enlisted men reported at the Parole Camp, and about 100 were absent, sick or unaccounted for. Of the regimental officers Maj. Knox was the only one present, the others being at Johnson's Island. There were about a dozen company officers present; each company, with the exception of *K*, having one or more representatives.

On Nov. 10th the regiment arrived at Meridian, Miss., having been assigned to Polk's Corps, Army of the Mississippi, Gen. Joseph E. Johnston, commanding.

Some of the non-commissioned officers of Co. K having requested to be restored to the ranks, the following reorganization was ordered: O. Sergt., Norman Cameron, 2d Sergt., Wm. H. Fay, 3d Sergt., C. Hardie Royals, 4th Sergt., M. D. Lamar, 5th Sergt., D. P. Smith, Corporals, E. L. Averhart, O. M. Blaylock, G. Hearn and J. D. Rice.

Lieut. Haley of Co. G was assigned to the command of Co. K, but was in a few weeks replaced by Lieut. Johnson, of Co. F.

The regiment was armed with new Austrian rifles, and the old routine of drill was once more resumed. Co. K made rapid progress and was complimented by Maj. Knox, by being excused from evening drill after Nov. 26th on account of its proficiency.

On Nov. 25th the regiment received two months' pay to April 30th, and on Dec. 4th, was paid to Oct. 31st, with all arrearages, including $50 bounty and commutation for clothing; about $125,000 was disbursed to the regiment at this time. A limited amount of clothing was also issued, and some shoes, but the latter were scarce, only 15 pairs to the regiment. Rations were of good quality, and much more plentiful than ever afterwards, consisting of corn meal and a little flour, beef, bacon, sweet potatoes, salt, vinegar and soap. Early in November orders were issued to build log barracks for winter quarters, 18 by 22 feet each designed for 25 men.

The regiment had been declared exchanged on Oct. 16th, but it was soon known in camp that the Federals had denied the validity of the exchange, disputes having arisen in regard to the cartel. In camp the subject was discussed with much interest, especially the question what would be our fate if recaptured by the enemy. Political questions of the day now crept into our camp fire discussions, especially the acts of the Confederate Congress relative to the army. The act restricting furloughs and other privileges and offering in lieu thereof increased pay, also the act forcing men who had put in substitutes to report for duty were subjects of debate, and the former was bitterly denounced.

# CHAPTER VIII.

Return of Co. K to Active Duty—Arrival at Mobile—A Flooded
Camp—Short of Ammunition—At Fort Gaines—Fishermen's
Spoils—Going to School—A Spy in Camp—In North Georgia.

The First Alabama Regiment was not required to do other duty than camp guard and drill until about the 1st of December; three companies of the regiment were then sent down the Mobile and Ohio Railroad to guard the bridges, and heavy details were made from the remaining companies—about 125 men daily—for provost duty at Meridian. This made it necessary for the men to go on duty every other day, and put an end to drilling. It was very severe on the few commissioned officers present, and their complaints finally led to the regiment being relieved of a portion of the burden.

December passed without any event of particular interest. On January 21, 1864, Cos. C, H and K were ordered to Jackson, Miss., and on the following morning took the cars, arriving at Jackson on the 23d. We went into camp on the east bank of Pearl River, opposite the city. Co. K had 33 men present for work. Shovels and picks were issued, guns stacked, and on Sunday morning, the 24th, the detail began grading a road down the bluff. The railroad bridge burned in the spring of 1863, not having been rebuilt, the intention was to make a road, so that locomotives and cars—of which there were a considerable number west of Pearl River—could be ferried across the river. The bluff being a hard clay marl, the progress was slow.

On February 3d, Gen. Sherman advanced from Vicksburg with 30,000 men and 60 pieces of artillery. On the 4th orders were issued to the three companies of the First Alabama to cook up three days' rations, and they were attached to the Tenth Texas Regiment, Ector's Brigade, French's Division.

As the Federals entered Jackson at sundown on the 5th, the Confederates evacuated the town and took the road to Brandon. The pontoon bridge was cut loose and floated down the river. After marching twelve miles, we halted till 4 A. M., when the retreat was resumed. Passing through Brandon at sunrise, the battalion took the road to Morton, where, on Sunday afternoon, we took the cars for Meridian, arriving during the night. The three companies stationed on the Mobile and Ohio Railroad proceeded to Mobile without rejoining the regiment, but the other companies remained at Meridian until the 14th, except the sick, who were sent with the regimental baggage to Demopolis by train on the 12th. When Meridian was evacuated, on the 14th, the First Alabama, owing to its excellent morale and discipline, was selected to form the rear guard of the retreating army. They marched to the Tombigbee River, where the First Alabama took the boat for Mobile, arriving on the 19th or 20th of February. Here the three detached companies from the Mobile and Ohio Railroad rejoined the command, and the regiment was, on the 22d, sent to the land defences and given charge of seven of the outer redans or forts. In two only of these were guns mounted, and nearly all were incomplete. It was thought that Mobile was Sherman's objective point, and a large force of negroes was at work on the outer line of fortifications, the inner lines being complete. Drilling, both in the heavy artillery and infantry school, was at once resumed. Co. K was stationed at Redan E, which was but just commenced. We remained here till March 8th, when the danger of an attack from Sherman having disappeared, the regiment was withdrawn from the lines and encamped on an open square on Government Street. The day following there was a heavy rain which flooded the camp, and portions of Government Street were knee-deep in water. In the tents the men piled their knapsacks and blankets on benches and such other articles of camp furniture as would keep them above water.

Orders were received on Sunday, March 13th, to cook up two days' rations, and to be ready to march at 9, A. M., on Monday, for Alabama Port. It was 3, P. M., when the regiment moved, and only nine miles were scored; but on the following day a march of twenty miles brought us to our destination. The Twenty-first Alabama was relieved, and on Wednesday started for Mobile. Two companies of the First Alabama were sent to Cedar Point to man the batteries there, while the others did picket duty along the coast and on Fowl River. The camp was on the bay in a pine grove. The men were furnished with tents, and were soon comfortably quartered. An abundance of oysters could be had by dredging for them, while at several of the picket posts the men could feast on bivalves all day. Under such circumstances, the duty imposed on the regiment was not regarded as onerous.

On the 25th of March four companies of the regiment were ordered down the coast to repel a raid of the enemy. It was necessary to collect all the cartridges from the remaining four companies to fill the boxes of those ordered away, as only twenty rounds per man had been issued to the regiment since its return to duty, and there was not a round in the ordnance wagon. Considering that the regiment had been acting as rear-guard of Polk's army, and had been sent down the bay to do picket duty, it was a remarkable state of affairs. The alarm proved a false one, and the detachment returned. On the 26th two companies were sent to Fort Powell; and on the 27th another company was ordered to Cedar Point, making three at that post. Co. K remained at Alabama Port. Lieut. Johnson, who had for sometime been in command of Co. K, was, on the 27th, relieved by order of Maj. Knox, by Lieut. Jones, of Co. I; this caused great dissatisfaction, as the latter was not liked. In a few days, however, he was furloughed, and Lieut. Crymes, of Co. I, a most gallant and popular gentleman, was placed in command. On the 1st of April our rations were increased—the meat from 1¼ pounds per day to 1½, and the bacon from ⅓ of a pound to ½ pound. The battalion of the regiment at Alabama Port was ordered, on the morning of April 5th, to strike tents, and at 8, A. M. started for Cedar Point, where a boat was in waiting to convey seven companies of the regiment to Fort Gaines, Dauphin Island, three being left at Fort Powell and Cedar Point. Only one-half of the men could be carried at one trip, and it was after dark when the second boat-load was landed. In the allotment of the guns of the fort to the regiment, Co. K fared badly; for though it was one of the four companies that served as heavy artillery at Port Hudson, and the only company that served exclusively as such during the siege, yet it was sent to the flanking casemates, while green companies were sent to the barbette guns. The Thirtieth Louisiana Regiment was on duty at the fort on alternate days with the first Alabama, but two companies of the First were sent into the fort every night to man the guns. About the only relief from the monotony of guard duty was the arrival of blockade runners, one or two of which came in each week. They would slip in quietly at night, and in the morning their low grey hulls could be seen lying under the guns of Fort Morgan.

On the 16th of April a scouting party of 100 men landed from the enemy's fleet on the western end of Dauphin Island, but were driven to their boats by a picket guard of ten men. The only other incident of our stay at Fort Gaines was on April 20th, when the C. S. gunboat "Gaines" ran out near Fort Morgan to practice with her guns. About the same time a Federal war ship began shelling a working party throwing up a battery near Fort Morgan. The men crowded the ramparts in the expectation of seeing a general engagement, as rumors had been in circulation for some time that Fort Morgan was to be bombarded; but quiet was soon restored. Co. I rejoined the regiment from Cedar Point on the 20th.

Fishing constituted the chief amusement of the men, and they met with great success. There was a large seine on the island, and with this wagon loads of fish were caught; but those of the best quality were brought in by the hook and line sportsmen—redfish, croakers, sea bass, blue cat, sand mullet, drum and sheepshead being on their strings. The seine was a dragnet for all kinds of monsters. On one occasion a sawfish 12 feet 10 inches long, and weighing 338 pounds, was caught; the sword or saw was 2 feet 10 inches in length and from 4 to 6 inches broad. On another occasion an immense sturgeon was hauled in; while among the smaller fry were sting rays, horseshoe crabs, sea nettles, sea porcupines and a variety of other curiosities. Porpoises were gamboling in the bay nearly all the time, and in the lagoons on the island were alligators.

May 3d, the regiment embarked on the steamboat "C. W. Durrance" for Mobile, where it was quartered in the State Press Warehouse. Co. I was sent to Dog River on the 4th, and on the 5th the other companies went to Pollard, Ala. Co. K was immediately ordered back to Hall's Landing on Tensas River, where it arrived on the 7th. Co. C was ordered to Greenville, and two companies were ordered to do picket duty on the railroad to Pensacola. The camp of Co. K was about one mile from Hall's Landing, and there it remained for two weeks. Lieut. Adams, who had been exchanged, joined the company about May 20th. On May 16th a number of officers and men were detailed from the regiment to attend an artillery school in Mobile. Of Co. K, Sergts. Cameron, Fay and Smith were selected. They reported, but before the school was fairly organized the regiment was ordered to North Georgia. The bill of fare at the school is worth of preservation:—Breakfast, rye coffee and corn bread (of unsifted meal); dinner, corn bread and boiled bacon, except on three days out often, when molasses was issued in lieu of bacon; supper, corn bread and rice boiled in the pot liquor left at noon. The order of exercises at the school was as follows:—Reveille, 5 A. M.; police, 5.10; drill in infantry and artillery, 5.30 to 6.30; breakfast, 7; guard mounting, 7.45; studies and recitations, 8 to 12 M.; dinner, 1 P. M.; studies and recitations, 2 to 4.30; infantry and artillery drill, 5 to 6; police, 6.10; dress parade, 6.30; supper, 7; tattoo, 9; taps, 9.30.

The detail rejoined the company on the 23d, and on the 24th the command took the cars for Montgomery; the other companies started a day or two earlier. During the six months that had elapsed since the company reassembled it had lost a number of its members. W. H. Hutchinson had been transferred to the cavalry, Wm. Douglass, E. Jenkins and Henry Fralick to the navy, and, as previously mentioned, Callens and Hays had died. While at Mobile and en route to North Georgia, the following recruits joined the company: A. D. Ellis, Autauga Co., February, 1864; — Harvey, March, 1864; George W. Gibbons, D. E. Holt and G. W. Hunt, Autauga Co., May, 1864. In June, while in North Georgia, the following recruits joined the company: A. G. Gresham, N. Landers, W. M. Trammel, of Tallapoosa Co., and Isaac Ward, Montgomery Co. Harvey, who joined the company at Mobile to avoid being conscripted, deserted before we left there. The writer called the attention of the officer in command of the company to the suspicious character of the man on the day that he enlisted, but there was nothing on which to base charges, and no notice was taken of the warning. Subsequent events demonstrated the correctness of the suspicion that he was a spy. He stated that he had been employed in the Mobile navy yard, and he was evidently familiar with the construction of the ram "Tennessee," as, in conversation, he explained how she could be disabled. The rudder-chains, he said, lay along the deck, protected only by a cast-iron shield, and they could easily be shot away. A few months later the "Tennessee"; was disabled in precisely the way he predicted. Whether he conveyed to the enemy the information of this weakness of an otherwise powerful vessel is a matter of conjecture, but it is certainly a singular coincidence.

The strength of Co. K at the beginning of the Tennessee campaign, including the new recruits, was probably about 62 men, of whom perhaps 40 were present for duty. Lieut. N. K. Adams was in command.

The company arrived at Montgomery on the morning of the 25th. A number of them who lived in Autauga County received twelve hours' furlough. The company left Montgomery on the morning of the 26th, and rejoined the regiment at New Hope Church, Saturday morning, May 28th. Knapsacks and other *impedimenta*, with the exception of blankets, were left in Montgomery.

# CHAPTER IX.

In North Georgia with Johnston and Hood—Retreat to Kennesaw—A
Gallant Deed—Hood's New Policy—Defending Atlanta—The
Valley of Death—The Gallant First—Fate of the Wounded—Death
of Sergt. Fay—Electing a Lieutenant—Evacuation of Atlanta—At
Lovejoy's Station.


The First Alabama Regiment, on its arrival in North Georgia, was attached to
Canty's Brigade, but was soon transferred to Quarles' Brigade (Tennessee troops),
Walthall's Division, Polk's Corps. The regiment, excepting Co. K, arrived in time
to take part in the battle of New Hope Church, on the 25th of May. When Co. K
reported, on the 28th, active skirmishing was in progress along the entire line of
Polk's Corps, and during the next few days the regiment lost a number of men,
among them being the Assistant Surgeon, Dr. Winnemore, who had an eye shot
out. To June 2d the loss was three killed and eight wounded in the regiment.

On the night of June 1st the regiment was withdrawn from the front to the reserve line, and on the following night the New Hope line was abandoned. For several days it had rained heavily, and the clay roads were badly cut up. At 10, P. M.,
the regiment moved into the road immediately in the rear of the artillery and wag-
on-train. Every few hundred yards the wagons or guns would stick in the mud,
and the infantry would be brought to a halt; but no opportunity was thus given
for rest, as the road was liquid mud, and not even the musket could be brought
to an "order." A drizzling rain added to the discomfort of the men. At daylight on
the morning of the 3d we halted near the foot of Lost Mountain, having marched
five miles in seven hours. Fires were kindled, a ration of whiskey distributed, and
the men were allowed to rest till after 12, noon, when the regiment was placed
in position. Breastworks were, as usual, at once constructed. Privates A. D. Ellis,
W. L. Ellis, John Griffin, Joseph Hurd and John Williamson were detailed at this
time, with others of the regiment, to act, till further orders, as sharpshooters. From
Lost Mountain the regiment moved to Pine Mountain, where it remained till June
18th. Daily rains made life in the trenches almost unendurable, and there was considerable sickness. Gen. Johnston did all he could to alleviate the discomforts of
the soldiers; abundant rations of corn-bread were issued, and occasionally a little
genuine coffee. Meat was scarce and of flour there was none.

On the night of the 18th of June the army fell back to the Kennesaw line of defence, and on the 19th entrenched. This night's march, like that of the retreat from
New Hope, was one long to be remembered. The road was ankle deep in mud and
water, with occasional holes waist-deep, full of thin mud. Into these the soldiers

would frequently stumble, requiring their comrades' help to get out. During the early part of the night there were showers, and early next morning, as the soldiers filed up the steep wooded slopes of Kennesaw, a heavy fog saturated their clothing. By 10, A. M., a line of works had been completed, and Co. K was then ordered to assist in dragging two pieces of artillery to the top of Kennesaw. The detail of sharpshooters was at the foot of the mountain, and was soon actively engaged skirmishing. On the 20th the line was under a terrific artillery fire, and A. D. Ellis, of Co. K, was seriously wounded by a fragment of shell. He rejoined the company at Tuscumbia. While stationed on Kennesaw, Sergt. Cameron performed a notable act of bravery; during a heavy artillery fire a shrapnel shell fell in the entrenchments amidst Co. K. Sergt. Cameron, without an instant's hesitation, seized the smoking missile and hurled it outside the works ere it exploded.

In the severe battle of June 27th, when Sherman attempted to break the Confederate lines, the enemy charged into the rifle-pits of Quarles' brigade, but were repulsed. Though under fire, the First Alabama was not closely engaged in this battle; its loss was trifling, and in Co. K there were no casualties. While on Kennesaw, Assistant-Surgeon Madding, of the First Alabama, was killed by a sharpshooter.

On the night of July 2d Gen. Johnston fell back from Kennesaw to the line south of Marietta. A portion of Co. K was on picket, but overtook the regiment without losing a man. Sherman followed close in pursuit, and when the new position was reached, no time was lost in entrenching. In less than thirty minutes from the time the First Alabama halted, the men had constructed temporary breastworks and were ready and eager for the fray. Sherman, however, finding Johnston prepared, contented himself with shelling our lines. The fire of the enemy's sharpshooters was very annoying, and on the 4th, Corp. James D. Rice was wounded by them. He rejoined the company prior to the Tennessee campaign.

About 9 P. M. on the night of the 4th, the army again retreated, the new line being that of the Chattahoochie River. Breastworks were again constructed, and here the regiment remained till another flank movement by Sherman compelled Gen. Johnston, on the 9th, to cross the river. The regiment was stationed on the line south of Peach Tree Creek. While here, Lieut. Adams was transferred to the Navy Department, Richmond; and an election in the company, held by order of Maj. Knox, resulted in the choice of Galvin Golsan as Second Lieutenant, Jr. Orderly-Sergt. Cameron was also brevetted First Lieutenant for gallantry, and, pending Lieut. Golsan's examination for a commission, was placed in command of the company.

Gen. Hood took command of the army on July 19th. By five o'clock on the morning of the 20th the sound of musketry on the right announced the inauguration of the new policy of aggressive instead of defensive warfare. The regiment was at this time deployed as skirmishers on Peach Tree Creek, three-quarters of a mile in front of the works. Orders were received to retire as skirmishers, and assemble on the main line. This was done under a heavy artillery fire, in good order. The brigade having, in the meantime, moved to the right, the regiment followed at a double quick, overtaking it in position on the reserve line immediately in the rear of the heaviest fighting. No call was made on the reserve, and at the close of the day the regiment returned to its former position, but was marching and countermarching all that night and the following day. On the night of the 21st the regiment was withdrawn to Atlanta, and placed on picket. Private Tharp was missing on the arrival of the company at its new post, and was not again heard from.

The usual work of entrenching was immediately begun, and in three hours everything was ready for an attack. Late on the afternoon of the 22d the regiment was ordered to the right to storm a twelve-gun battery; but Hood's attack had failed, and the order was countermanded when the regiment was in position. It bivouacked there for the night, and on the following morning returned to its former position. Here it remained till July 27, when it was withdrawn 300 yards to the rear for rest. The same evening, however, the regiment was ordered to fall in, with blankets rolled, ready for marching, and it remained in line all night awaiting further orders. It rained gently through the night, but when morning came the clouds disappeared, and the sun rose bright and clear—for the last time for many of the brave men of the First Alabama.

About 10, A. M., came the command, "Attention!" "Right face!" "Forward, march!" After marching two or three miles, the command was halted till about 3, P. M., when it was again ordered forward. Soon the sound of musketry announced that a battle was in progress immediately in front. Hood, with Stewart's and Lee's corps, was attempting to break through the enemy's line near the Lickskillet, or Poorhouse Road. Gen. Quarles at once placed his brigade in line of battle—the First Alabama on the left, Co. K to the left of the color company—Brevet-Lieut. Cameron in command, Lieut. Golsan, who had not yet received his commission, accompanying him. In a few minutes the brigade was under fire, and, pressing forward, passed over Canty's brigade, which was lying down, and, crossing a rail fence, charged down a slope—

> "Into the jaws of death,
> Into the mouth of hell."

No sooner had they reached the foot of the hill, crossed a small run or brook and begun to ascend the opposite side, than a withering flanking fire swept down their ranks; while from the works in front, halfway up the ascent and hidden in the edge of the woods, streamed forth a constant blaze of musketry, while shots from the artillery pierced the bank of smoke like flashes of lightning. Still the men made no halt, but, with heads bent down as though breasting the cyclone, pressed onward, till Gen. Quarles, seeing that none could survive to reach the enemy's lines, gave the order to halt and fall back to the run, now red with blood, where a slight cover was afforded. They were within fifty yards of the enemy when halted, and a gallant soldier of another command was buried by the enemy where he fell just outside their works, and his grave, carefully protected, was marked by them with a tribute to his bravery. The charge was made over open ground, while the enemy were wholly concealed in the woods and behind a breastwork constructed of a rail fence and rock piled up. Lieut. Golsan fell early in the fight, and Lieut. Cameron just before reaching the run at the foot of the hill. Both were cheering on the men when stricken down. Co. K lost 19 men killed and wounded out of 32 engaged, the casualties being as follows:—

Killed—Brev. First Lieut. Norman Cameron; Junior Second Lieut. Galvin Golsan; Privates William Dubose and John Owens: total, 4.

Mortally wounded—Privates A. C. Smyth, J. J. Stuart, and A. J. Thompson: total, 3.

Seriously wounded—Sergt. M. D. Lamar; Privates John Boggan, George Durden, E. Leysath, J. L. Simpson and John Williamson: total, 6.

Severely wounded—Corpls. E. L. Averheart and O. M. Blaylock; Private C. B. Brown: total, 3.

Slightly wounded (not sent to hospital)—Privates J. C. Hearn, John Tunnell and J. H. Shaver: total, 3.

Of the regiment, 171 men, out of 325 present, were killed and wounded, including 13 color-bearers. It was not till about dark that the shattered remnant of the First Alabama was withdrawn. The names of those of Co. K who escaped unharmed from this terrible gorge are, to the best of the writer's knowledge—Sergt. W. H. Fay; Corp. G. W. Hearn; Privates T. M. Boggan, W. L. Ellis, W. W. Day, John Griffin, Joseph Hurd, G. W. Hunt, R. H. Kirkpatrick, John Killough, Joseph May, Eli T. Sears and Josiah Tunnell.

Of the wounded, Privates Smyth and Thomson lived till they reached the hospital at Griffin, where both died. There is some uncertainty in regard to J. J. Stuart's fate, several members of the company asserting positively that he was mortally wounded in this battle, and died in hospital; others, having equally good opportunities of knowing the facts, being ignorant of his fate; and some asserting that he was not present. His name does not appear in a memoranda of the killed and wounded made about ten days after the battle by the writer, who was himself in Montgomery, Ala., at the time. Sergt. Lamar received a bullet in the hip and was never able to return to duty. Private Williamson received a bullet in the shoulder, a second in the thigh, while a third chipped a piece off of a front tooth. He, too, was permanently disabled, as were Durden, Leysath and Simpson. The others soon recovered of their wounds. For some days doubt existed as to Lieut. Cameron's death, but the lingering hope was dispelled by a member of another company, who saw him breathe his last. Lieut. Golsan's body was carried a little distance to the rear by some of the company; but they had to leave him, and with the other dead he was buried by the enemy. There was no foundation whatever for the rumor, which reached his home, that he was not killed.

Maj. Knox was seriously wounded, and the command of the regiment devolved upon Capt. Williams. Sergt. W. H. Fay was ordered to take command of Co. K. The brigade bivouacked for the night near the battle-field, and on the 29th returned to its former position on the defences, and the regiment resumed picket duty.

While out on picket, August 3d, Co. K suffered another great loss. Private

Farmer was slightly wounded, and expressing a desire for water, Sergt. Fay volunteered to get some at a neighboring well. He took several canteens, and succeeded in reaching the well in safety; but on his return, while crossing an exposed opening, a ball pierced his heart. He exclaimed, "Oh, men! oh, men!" walked about fifteen steps and sat down under the shade of a small tree; and as Sergt. Royals, who ran to his assistance, caught him in his arms, he struggled once or twice and died. Thus perished, in the glory of early Christian manhood, one of the pure and noble of earth. The company thus lost in less than one week two officers commanding, and one who had been elected to command — three noble, Christian men, Cameron, Golsan, and Fay.

On the death of Sergt. Fay, Sergt. C. H. Royals took command, and held it till relieved by Lieut. Jones, of Co. I. Private G. F. Martin was slightly wounded on the 4th. On the 12th of August Private D. E. Holt was severely wounded, a Minie ball passing through both thighs, but fortunately missing the larger blood-vessels and bones. He was taken to the hospital, where gangrene getting into the wound, he narrowly escaped death, and was disabled from further service.

An election for Junior Second Lieutenant was held on August 9th. John L. Alexander received 9 votes, and Daniel P. Smith 10. Lieut. Smith soon after successfully passed his examination for promotion, but did not receive his commission till September 7th. John L. Alexander was about this time made Orderly Sergeant. Corpls. Averheart and Hearn were promoted to sergeantcies, and Josiah Tunnell and G. H. Royals were appointed corporals.

While at Atlanta, those of the soldiers who had any money could purchase some few articles of luxury; rice could be bought for 75 cents per pound, and flour for 50 cents per pound. The rations, as usual, consisted of corn bread and beef.

On August 19th the regiment was ordered down the railroad to intercept a raid, but went into camp in the outskirts of Atlanta. Again, on the 21st, the regiment was sent three or four miles to the right of the Confederate lines, where it constructed an abattis. The following day it was ordered back to its old position at the breastworks near the Chattanooga Railroad. On the night of the 25th the Federals withdrew from around Atlanta, moving to the south; and on the morning of the 26th Gen. Stewart's corps occupied the abandoned works. The First Alabama, with other troops, advanced to the Chattahoochie on a reconnaissance, without meeting the enemy. In the afternoon the regiment was withdrawn, and camped inside the city lines. Here we remained until the morning of the 31st, when we were ordered down the Macon Railroad towards East Point, some four or five miles. During the day the regiment was mustered for pay. Towards evening the command returned to Atlanta, camping beside the Macon Railroad. Early on the morning of Thursday, September 1, the First Alabama was sent out on the Poorhouse or Lickskillet road on picket, being stationed about half a mile from the battle-field of July 28th. Rations of hard tack, all that the men could carry, were here given out. Returning to the city (leaving the picket line at 10.45 P. M.), we found it evacuated with the exception of the cavalry rear-guard. On an open square a huge pile of cotton was fiercely blazing, while down the Macon Railroad heavy explosions told of the destruction of an ammunition train abandoned through the negligence of the

Chief Quartermaster. The First Alabama, which formed the infantry portion of the rear-guard, made no halt in the city, but took the road to McDonough, passing out of the city limits about 1 or 2 o'clock on the morning of the 2d. Except for brief intervals of rest, the march was continued till noon on the 2d, when the command deployed and built breastworks. Just as these were completed, orders were received to take the road again. At 10.45, P. M., another halt was made, and the men were allowed to rest till 2.30, A. M., Saturday, when they were ordered into line, but no move was made till daylight. About 3, P. M., a halt was made four or five miles from Lovejoy's Station. Sunday morning, the 4th, the regiment marched four or five miles, and deployed in a piece of thick woods. Sharp firing could be heard in front, and occasionally a cannon ball went crashing through the trees; but the firing soon ceased, and the regiment went into camp.

There were twenty-two men present in Co. K when the retreat from Atlanta began. Two or three, Private Hurd among the number, broke down on the march, and were sent to hospitals. Lieut. Jones, of Co. I, assigned to the command of Co. K, was left behind in Atlanta, and Lieut. Smith took command of the company on the night of the 1st, though not commissioned till the 7th.

# CHAPTER X.

Hood's Raids on Sherman's Railroad Communications—Finding Lost Mountain—Hold the Fort—Tearing up Railroads—In Alabama—A Dismal Night—Review of the Army—Foraging in Tennessee—Catching Mud Larks.

The First Alabama remained in camp at Lovejoy's till Sunday, September 18th, a camp-ground was cleared up in the woods, and drilling was resumed. During the Atlanta campaign the cooking was done at the wagon-yards; now, cooking utensils were issued, and the men were enabled to have comparatively decent fare. W. L. Ellis was detailed to go to Montgomery after the company's knapsacks, and also to procure clothing from home for the men. On the afternoon of the day he left orders were received to cook up two days' rations, and at noon on the 18th the command broke camp and marched to Fayetteville, a distance of ten miles. At 2 o'clock Monday morning the reveille sounded, but it was 5.30, A. M., before the march was resumed. At dark the regiment bivouacked three miles beyond Palmetto, having marched eighteen miles.

On Tuesday, after a march of five miles, the command was deployed and orders given to entrench. The position was four or five miles from the Chattahoochie and about twenty-five miles from Atlanta. While camped near Palmetto, on Monday morning, September 26th, President Davis informally reviewed the army, being greeted along portions of the line by cries of "Give us Johnston!"

Thursday, September 29th, the command again received orders to march. Private W. L. Ellis arrived that morning with the company baggage and boxes from home, and a hasty distribution had to be made of the contents of the latter. Clean clothing from the knapsacks was donned, the baggage repacked and sent into Palmetto to a private house for storage; it was never seen again.

At noon the command started, crossing the Chattahoochie that evening on a pontoon bridge at the Pumpkintown, or Phillips, Ferry, and going into camp after a march of eight miles. It was showery on the 30th, but a march of ten miles was made on the Powder Springs Road. October set in stormy, the rain falling all day and night, the command remaining in camp. A march of twelve miles on Sunday, the 2d, brought the regiment to familiar scenes, and it bivouacked three miles from Lost Mountain. The troops recognized their old battlegrounds, and there was no little enthusiasm aroused. After a march of ten miles on the 3d, the command struck the railroad at Big Shanty Station, which was captured, with a few prisoners, after a slight skirmish.

Our division (Walthall's) was deployed along the track, which was torn up, ties piled and burned, and the rails—heated red hot—bent. This work continued till 3 o'clock on the morning of the 4th. After a few hours' rest, the division moved up the road, tearing up the track and burning the ties. At noon, tired and hungry—being without rations—the regiment took the road towards Lost Mountain, and went on picket five miles from Big Shanty Station. A march of seven miles was made on the 5th, and just at dark the brigade began the ascent of Lost Mountain, the regiment going on picket near the top. The mountain side was thickly carpeted with prickly pear, and falls and ejaculations more forcible than pious were frequent. On the 6th the command marched twelve miles, passing the site of New Hope Church.

Near New Hope, French's shattered division, repulsed the previous day at Allatoona Bridge, was met. Gen. French's assault on the fort at Allatoona was of the most desperate character, and resulted in placing half his command *hors du combat*. Gen. Sherman, marching to the relief of the beleaguered garrison, signaled from the top of Kennesaw Mountain to its commander that despatch made memorable by Bliss's hymn:—

"Hold the fort, I am coming.

W. T. SHERMAN."

The arrival of the Federal troops forced the Confederates to retire just as they were about to reap the fruit of their tremendous sacrifices.

Thus far it had rained every day since the army left Palmetto, but the 7th was pleasant, the roads were good, and a march of fifteen miles was made towards Van Wirt. Another march of fifteen miles on the 8th brought the regiment to Cedartown. This ended Hood's first raid on the railroad; ten or twelve miles of track had been torn up, and about 400 prisoners taken. The First Alabama did not load their guns. Co. K lost one man—Sergt. George Hearn—who was barefoot, and on the night that the regiment ascended Lost Mountain was left behind, captured, and sent to Rock Island, Ill.

At noon on the 9th orders were received to march; the left wing of the First Alabama, including Co. K, was the brigade rear guard, and did not get into camp until 10.30, P. M., after a march of twelve miles. On the 10th the Coosa River was crossed at Coosaville, on a pontoon bridge, the day's progress being ten or twelve miles. Eighteen miles were scored on the 11th, on the Dirt-town road, and on the 12th over twenty miles, the regiment camping at 9, P. M., three miles from Resaca. Soon after bivouacking it began to rain. An attack on Resaca having failed, that post was flanked, and the railroad struck at Tilton at noon on the 13th, which post surrendered to Gen. French. The track was torn up all the way to Dalton, the ties burned, and rails bent. Dalton surrendered to Gen. Cheatham with about 1,000 prisoners without a fight. The First Alabama did good service tearing up track, and camped that night two miles south of Dalton. On the 14th Rocky Face Mountain was crossed at Dug Gap, and after marching twelve miles the regiment went into camp. The route on the 15th lay through the Chattooga Valley for eighteen miles. Passing through Treadwell Gap and across Chattooga River, the regiment, after a march of ten miles, bivouacked on the evening of the 16th, two miles beyond Summerville, Ga.

The second raid resulted in the capture of about 1,500 or 2,000 prisoners and the destruction of twenty miles of railroad track. Co. K had no more stragglers, but the men were weary and footsore, having, since leaving Palmetto, marched some two hundred miles in seventeen days.

On the 17th, at 2, A. M., the command again broke camp, and marching ten miles halted for the day at sunrise. The army crossed the state line of Alabama on the 18th, passed through Gaylesville, and camped three miles beyond, having marched fifteen miles. Fifteen miles were scored again on the 19th, the route taking us past the Round Mountain Iron Works, in Cherokee County. Reveille sounded at an early hour on the 20th, and by 3, A. M., the regiment was on the road; twenty miles were made by 2, P. M., when we camped five miles beyond Gadsden. A welcome rest of forty-four hours was here allowed the soldiers, and on the 21st some clothing was issued to those most in need. Another treat was the distribution of a large army mail, the accumulation of two weeks or more. The order to march was given at 3, A. M., on the 22d, but it was countermanded before we had gone three hundred yards, and it was 10, A. M., before the final start was made; fifteen miles were, however, accomplished before camping, the route being over Lookout Mountain. The army crossed the Black Warrior River on the 23d, and, passing through Brooksville, added seventeen miles to the march record. Though the road was very rocky, a march of seventeen miles was also made on the 24th; the town of Summit was the only point of interest. On the 25th the regiment marched thirteen miles to Somerville, and on the 26th thirteen miles to the lines around Decatur, a total of one hundred and thirty-five miles in ten days, including two days' rest at Gadsden.

A brisk cannonade was in progress when the regiment arrived, and it was at once ordered to the picket line. It had been raining at intervals all day, and the night closed in cold and gloomy. When the picket line was reached it was quite dark. At 10, P. M., an order was received to advance the line one hundred and fifty yards and dig rifle pits. It was impossible to see more than five feet in any direction, and as the command was deployed as skirmishers, the movement was executed with considerable difficulty, but the new line was at last formed. About the time the rifle pits were completed, the men supplementing the few entrenching tools with tin-cups and pans, the rain came pouring down, filling the pits and converting the whole ground into a marsh. The men were so exhausted that so soon as the rain had ceased and they had bailed out the pits all but those on guard lay down in the mud and fell asleep.

At daylight skirmishers were ordered forward, but finding the enemy in force they fell back to the picket line with a loss of one man mortally wounded in Co. E. Soon after daylight the regiment was relieved and rejoined the brigade. It rained at intervals all day, and to add to the discomfort of the soldiers no rations were issued except a little beef; there was no bread for two or three days. At this time began the private foraging, which later proved so disastrous to the discipline of the army.

On the morning of October 29, the regiment left Decatur and marched sixteen miles westward, along the Memphis and Charleston Railroad, camping three miles east of Courtland. The line of march on the 30th was through a level, fertile country, but desolated by Federal raids, nearly every plantation building having been burned. We camped that night at Leedam, having marched fifteen miles and passed during the day through Courtland and Jonesboro. On the 31st a march of ten miles brought the regiment to Tuscumbia. The march record from September 29th now footed up three hundred and eighty-five miles.

For several days after arriving at Tuscumbia it was rainy; it then cleared off cold. On Sunday, November 6th, there was a general review and inspection, and on the 12th Gen. Beauregard reviewed the army, which, at that time, was said to number about 30,500 men. In Stewart's Corps there were 9,000 men. Corp. Rice and Privates A. D. Ellis and J. W. May rejoined the company on November 2d, and Junius Robinson on the 4th, making a total of 20 muskets. Our number was reduced by several sick sent to the rear before we crossed the Tennessee.

Monday, November 14th, the regiment marched to Florence and went into camp, and on the 18th received several months' pay, the first since leaving Meridian. At this muster there were present Lieut. Smith, O. Sergt. J. L. Alexander, Sergts. C. H. Royals and E. L. Averheart, Corps. J. D. Rice and Josiah Tunnell, and Privates T. M. Boggan, C. W. Brown, W. W. Day, A. D. Ellis, W. L. Ellis, E. Hearn, J. C. Hearn, J. Killough, J. W. May, G. F. Martin, Wm. Moncrief and John Tunnell. Private Martin, during the entire campaign, was detailed at the wagon camp as cook.

One great want of the army when it started on this campaign in the depth of winter was that of shoes. At the outset there were not a few who had but apologies for shoes, and when Hood reached the Tennessee River on his retreat, no less than 3,000 barefooted men straggled in the rear, literally leaving a trail of blood along the frozen pikes. The lack of rations was another serious misfortune; for a month prior to entering upon the campaign the troops had been on short rations of a miserable quality. Three-quarters of a pound of very coarse cornmeal and one pound of fresh beef, bone and all—and generally the bone predominated—nominally constituted a day's rations. These rations were issued at the wagon-yards or camps, where details from the companies cooked them. The beef was boiled and the meal, wet up with cold water and made into "pones," was browned—not cooked—in "Dutch ovens." Thus prepared, the food was distributed—company commissioned officers and men sharing alike—the bread, three days' rations at a time, the beef every day. By the time it reached the company the ration had so "shrunk in the pot" that the writer has seen a lean and lank Confederate dispose of his three days' rations of bread and one of beef at one sitting. All the army had chronic diarrhœa, and all were hungry. As a consequence of this latter fact, when the rich fields of Tennessee—the "land of hog and hominy"—were reached, no discipline could restrain the men, and thousands at a time were scattered through the country searching for something to satisfy their hunger. Company officers, themselves half-starved, sympathized with their men, and would not have punished them for foraging had it been possible; but what punishment could be inflicted upon men who were marching from early morn till night? "Mud Lark," as skinned hog meat was called by the soldiers—who even in their suffering still indulged in jokes—was brought in every night; six hundred pounds was captured one night by the foragers of the "First." The Regimental Commissary, who was on the lookout, seized it and compelled a *pro rata* distribution; but no other notice was taken of the offence. Parched corn augmented the scanty ration of bread, and, after marching all day, half the night would be spent by the hungry men in cooking up what had been gathered along the road or after camping.

In spite of the many hardships which our company had endured, the men, when they crossed the Tennessee, marching northward, were cheerful and willing for any duty or danger, and this was the spirit in the regiment and army.

A commander never uttered a more unfounded libel against his soldiers than Gen. Hood when he published that his troops were demoralized and could not be trusted in battle. Even when his half-starved legions left one-fourth their number on the battle-field of Franklin, after fighting for hours against a superior force, strongly entrenched, and at one time penetrating the enemy's line, he was not satisfied, but is reported to have said, in private conversation, that if his old Texas brigade had been with him he would have won the battle. In his book, however, he gave the troops who fought at Franklin a scanty meed of praise.

# CHAPTER XI.



It was raining slowly as, on Sunday, November 20, the First Alabama formed and marched down to the Tennessee river, crossed the long pontoon bridge, and went into camp four miles beyond. Monday, there was a light fall of snow, and the command advanced but seven miles. At night it turned off very cold, and Tuesday morning the roads were frozen hard. During the day the army crossed the State line of Tennessee, marked by a rough board sign placed by the roadside, every regiment cheering heartily, Tennessee troops being especially enthusiastic. The day's march was thirteen miles. Wednesday saw us twelve miles on our journey. The day was cold and wintry, and the soldiers, thinly clad and generally without overcoats, suffered keenly. It was slightly warmer on Thursday. As on Wednesday, the route lay through a hostile, mountainous country, and the slow progress made by the artillery and wagon trains, as well as the necessity of keeping the men well closed up, delayed the army, and only twelve miles were made. The mountaineers were mostly Union men, and showed no mercy to stragglers, either killing them outright or horribly maltreating them. On Friday the roads were better; the mountains were behind us; and as the troops passed through Henryville they were met with friendly greetings. The First Alabama went into camp two miles beyond Henryville, having marched fifteen miles, the best score since crossing the river. Saturday, the people were still more cordial, and the troops were cheered at Mount Pleasant. Sixteen miles had been tramped when the First went into camp eight miles from Columbia. On Sunday, the 27th, Stewart's corps arrived at Columbia, invested by Lee's corps the preceding day. At dusk the First Alabama were sent to the skirmish line. During the night the enemy evacuated the town, taking position on the other side of Duck River. The regiment remained in camp Monday. Gen. Forrest crossed four miles above Columbia on that day; and, a pontoon bridge having been put down, Cheatham's and Stewart's corps and Johnson's division of Lee's corps followed on the 29th. Schofield at once withdrew, and now began a spirited race for Franklin on parallel roads, the Federals having the advantage of holding the regular pike, while the Confederates marched over rough by-roads and through the fields. There was brisk skirmishing throughout the day between the flankers; but Cheatham, who had forged far enough ahead to have thrown his corps across the pike, failed to execute Hood's positive orders to do so. Hood then ordered Stewart's corps to the front to make the attack, but by the time they got up it was dark, and the men could not be got into proper position to ensure success. The two corps bivouacked at Spring Hill, and Schofield's army, unmolested, filed by so near that their wagons could be heard on the stony pike. This blunder lost Hood the Tennessee campaign. Gen. Hood states that Gen. Cheatham afterwards magnanimously acknowledged his error. Even Hood did not place any blame upon the army for this failure to attack. The soldiers were greatly fatigued after the twenty miles' march of the day; but would have gallantly responded to the order to attack, and themselves wondered why it was not given.

On the morning of November 30th the race was renewed, but Schofield had the advantage of being ahead of his foes. He was so hardly pushed, however, that he was obliged to sacrifice a considerable portion of his wagon train, overturning and burning the wagons or cutting down the wheels, and shooting the animals whenever they blocked the retreat of the infantry. In some cases whole teams could be seen lying dead in the traces. At another point a quartermaster's wagon had been overturned, and for rods around the road and fields were strewn with blankets. About noon, when four miles south of Franklin, the Federal cavalry deployed along a wooded crest running at right angles to the Columbia pike, and covered the wearied infantry while filing into the entrenchments at Franklin.

These entrenchments had been carefully constructed, and had already received their baptism of blood the year prior (April 10, 1863), when Gen. Van Dorn attacked Gen. Granger and was repulsed. The inner line was a regularly constructed earthwork, with a ditch on the outside about three feet deep and five feet wide. From the bottom of the ditch to the top of the parapet was at least six or seven feet. Heavy timbers or head logs crowned the top of the parapet, space being left between the logs and earth to allow the soldiers to fire. An abattis of black locust protected the front. Two hundred and fifty or three hundred yards in front of this—an open field with gentle slope intervening—was another connected line of earthworks, made by digging a ditch about eighteen inches or two feet in depth, and throwing the earth to the front. Outside of this, again, were detached rifle pits. This was the nature of the works on each side the Columbia pike, where the heaviest fighting took place. The works extended around Franklin in a semi-circle, touching Big Harpeth River above and below the town, a length of a mile and a half.

As Stewart's corps, which was in the advance, came up, the Federal cavalry also withdrew into Franklin. The Confederate forces rapidly deployed, Stewart's corps forming the right and Cheatham's the left, Johnston's division of Lee's corps being still in the rear. Stewart's corps was formed in line of battle between the Nashville and Decatur Railroad and the Lewisburg pike, about one and a quarter miles from Franklin and three-quarters of a mile from the Union lines. The corps was so fronted that an advance would take it across the railroad, striking the enemy's main line near the Columbia pike. Walthall's division was in the centre, with Quarles' brigade on the right. In front of Walthall was a deep cut in the railroad, which was not discovered till the advance had begun, and which necessitated his moving by the left flank, as subsequently stated, to avoid the obstacle. Much straggling had been caused by the forced marches of the two preceding days, and probably not over 15,000 or 16,000 men of Stewart's and Cheatham's corps were engaged in the battle, and Johnston's division, say 2,000 or 3,000 men, did not take part till the main attack had failed, about 7, P. M. The artillery, with the exception of a section of two Napoleon guns, did not participate in the battle. Forrest's cavalry was held in reserve on the flanks, Gen. Forrest himself being with the infantry during the charge.

Gen. Schofield's force was composed of the Fourth Corps, which was officially reported ten days after the battle to have numbered 14,172 men, the Twenty-third Corps, 10,207 men, and the Forty-fourth Missouri and Seventy-second Illinois unassigned. A Federal officer present stated that they had more men than could stand at the works, the lines being in some places six deep, those in rear loading for those in front.

The spirit of the Confederate troops, while not enthusiastic, was good. While waiting the completion of the formation, the men of the regiments first in line were quietly discussing the probable issue of the impending battle; some with an eye to the future were picking white beans from the dead vines in a field in our front; others, no less industrious, were eating every crumb in their haversacks. Among the latter was poor Brown of Co. K, who, on being remonstrated with for his imprudence, replied that he would be killed; his forebodings proved too correct; one hour later he was dead.

About half-past three the command "Attention!" ran quietly along Stewart's lines; a detail was ordered to the front to throw down a rail fence, and then came the orders "Forward!" "Double quick!" For two hundred yards the advance was through a corn-field, the dead stalks of which, of giant dimensions, were crossed and interlaced in every direction. When the farther side of the field was reached the command was halted, moved by the flank to the left, and the alignment corrected. The enemy's works were now in full view, and not over a half mile distant. Immediately in the front of the First Alabama there was a valley with a small stream of water at the bottom, the descent and ascent on the other side being quite sharp. An open grove of sugar maples, entirely free of underbrush, extended to the Federal rifle pits. Away to the right the rattle of musketry showed that the battle had begun, and the order, "Skirmishers to the front!" almost immediately followed. The latter moved rapidly forward, availing themselves of the cover of the large maples and firing slowly as they advanced. As yet not a bullet had whistled by us, and it was hard to realize that it was more than a skirmish drill, with such precision did the men move.

By the time the skirmishers were fifty yards away there came the orders, "Forward! Double quick!" Down the hill, across the brook, up the slope, over the railroad; then came the first deadly Yankee greeting—a shrapnel bursting in the ranks of Co. E, killing and wounding nine men. In three minutes more the space was covered, the Confederates were past the rifle pits and in the outer line of the enemy's works. Most of the Federals occupying them surrendered and were sent to the rear; many of those who tried to run back to the main line were shot down.

For an instant the line was halted and the men lay down in the captured works. Not a stump nor a stone obstructed the open field, on the farther side of which, behind their entrenchments, lay the main body of the enemy. To the right the roll of musketry was unintermitted, but immediately in our front, except from the Federal artillery, there was a momentary lull. It was but for a moment, then the order "Forward!" was repeated down the line. The men sprang to their feet, for the first time in the battle gave the "rebel yell," and dashed forward, corps, division, and brigade officers leading in the assault. At the same instant a sheet of smoke shot out from the earthworks in front, thickening, as volley after volley poured forth, into a great white bank, but broken every moment by tongues of flame from the cannon. Looming up above the smoke in shadowy form, like some old tower, just inside the enemy's works, were the huge timbers of a cotton-press; this was the only landmark; all else was hidden. But few shots were fired by the Confederates as they dashed forward, for, though there were no orders, each man instinctively felt that this was to be a struggle man to man. Two Napoleon guns, run forward by hand on the Columbia pike, kept well up with the line of battle and were fired steadily. No other artillery on the Confederate side fired a shot. The roar of the Federal musketry was something never to be forgotten; not even the Napoleons, nor the siege guns, firing from the fort on the other side of the river, could be heard distinct from that terrific volume of sound; yet the Confederates moved forward towards this death-dealing bank of smoke with all the precision of battalion drill. At the distance of forty yards from the works the Confederate line was unbroken and had suffered comparatively little loss. The effect of this solid, steady charge was such that Federal officers afterwards acknowledged that they could with difficulty keep their men from going to the rear. When within forty yards the enemy's fire began to tell, and the Confederates fell rapidly. The enemy fired remarkably low, due, it is said, to their simply laying their muskets on the slope of the parapet and pulling the trigger without exposing themselves to take aim. At last the ditch was reached; some of the assailants dashed through the embrasures of the battery; others tried to clamber over the parapet, and others exchanged shots with the Federals under the head logs. Men were brained with butts of muskets or bayonetted on the parapet, while the flanking fire of the angles soon filled the ditch with the dead and dying; a few got inside of the works unscathed and were taken prisoners. Just to the left of the pike the Confederates broke the Federal line, and for a short time held one of their batteries, but the Federal reserve charged, and after a desperate struggle regained possession. This was the situation at dark: the opposing forces confronting one another, with but a bank of earth between, like two stags of the forest head to head and antlers locked. Johnston's division coming up at 7, P. M., made a gallant effort to turn the evenly-balanced scale, but only added to Hood's already appalling losses. About 9, P. M., the firing slackened and the roar of musketry gradually died away, but was renewed at intervals as one or the other side perceived or suspected some movement of its foe.

So soon as the Federals were satisfied that the assault was over, they commenced quietly to withdraw, and by 3 o'clock the next morning they were safely across the river.

Daylight revealed to the Confederates their fearful loss; in front of some portions of the works the ground was covered with the dead. Report at the time placed the Confederate loss at 1,500 killed and 3,000 wounded. Hood, in his despatches from the battle-field, gave his loss at 4,500 killed, wounded and prisoners, the last being estimated at 1,000. Swinton, the historian, gives the Confederate loss as 1,739 killed, 3,850 wounded and 702 prisoners; total, 6,201. This would, in a measure, agree with Hood's own statement in "Advance and Retreat," where he places his total losses from all causes, from November 6th to December 10th, 7,547; this includes the losses at Columbia and in Forrest's skirmishes. It will thus be seen that nearly one-third of those engaged were killed and wounded, and that one-tenth were killed. Probably there never was a battle fought on the American continent, between civilized armies, where the slaughter was so great as in Hood's army. The Federals reported their loss at 189 killed, 1,033 wounded and 1,104 prisoners; total, 2,326. Their report of killed is, in the writer's opinion, understated, though the total may be correct. It was reported at the time that 300 Federal dead lay in the rear of the centre, where the heaviest fighting took place.

The casualties among the Confederate general officers were unparalleled, and their reckless exposure of their lives was the general subject of comment in the army. Nearly all went into the charge mounted, and Gens. Cleburne and Adams were killed while trying to spur their horses over the breastworks. Maj.-Gen. P. R. Cleburne and Brig.-Gens. Gist, John Adams, Strahl and Granberry were killed; Maj.-Gen. Brown and Brig.-Gens. Carter, Marrigault, Quarles, Cockrell and Scott wounded, and Brig.-Gen. Gordon was captured. Of Gen. Quarles' staff all were killed and wounded but the General's son, a lad of fourteen, who seized the brigade flag when the color-bearer fell, and bore it inside the enemy's works. Dismounted in the melee, he tore the flag from the staff, concealed it under his coat and got safely out with it.

Of Co. K, eleven men went into the charge; of these, two were killed, four wounded and two taken prisoners. Private C. W. Brown was shot through the heart, Private J. W. May was killed on breastworks by the butt of a musket, Lieut. Smith received a ball in the face, breaking the lower jaw, when near the main line of the enemy; Sergt. C. H. Royals was shot in the knee in the ditch and captured, but left behind when the enemy retreated; Serg. Averheart was wounded in the abdomen by a pistol bullet; Corp. Tunnell was shot through one thigh and across the other; Private W. L. Ellis was captured in the ditch, and Private J. C. Hearn sprang through the embrasure of the battery and was captured inside the enemy's lines. He relates that he placed his hand on the 12-pounder as he went in, and that it was so hot that it burned him. Corp. Rice and Privates A. D. Ellis and John Killough escaped unhurt. Of the members of Co. K not in the charge three were detailed, three were in the rear, footsore, barefoot or sick, and one—E. Hearn—had accidentally shot himself through the hand. A singular fatality followed the members of the Brown family in Co. K. There were three brothers—A. Pinkney, Elnathan and C. Wesley Brown—and a brother-in-law, J. A. Fergerson. The first two died of disease, and the last two were killed in battle. All were good men and brave, reliable soldiers. A fourth brother—Richard—who belonged to another command, lost an arm in battle. The loss in the regiment was about 150 out of 300 engaged. The color-guard were all killed or wounded. Lieut. Crymes, of Co. I, went over the entrenchments, and, refusing to surrender, was shot dead while waving his sword and calling to his men to follow. Maj. Knox was mortally wounded, Capt. Williams was taken prisoner, and the command of the remnant of the regiment devolved upon Lieut. McRae.

Corp. Rice collected together, on the morning after the battle, six men of Co. K, viz.: Privates T. M. Boggan, Day, A. D. Ellis, Killough, Martin and John Tunnell, and proceeded with the regiment to Nashville, where, some days later, O. Sergt. Alexander and private Moncrief rejoined the command.

Companies C and K were now united, and Orderly-Sergt. Alexander, of Co. K, was placed in command; Sergt. Blaylock, of Co. C, being second. The weather was extremely cold, and as nearly all the remnant of Co. K were barefoot and thinly clad, they suffered severely.

On December 15th, the first day of the battle of Nashville, Stewart's corps occupied the left of Hood's army. The First Alabama was stationed on the left flank of the corps, at right angles to the main line, behind a stone wall on the Hillsboro' pike. In response to a call for sharpshooters, Sergt. Alexander detailed T. M. Boggan, Killough and Moncrief to go to an outlying redoubt on the extreme left. The ground was covered with snow and ice. Late in the evening the enemy advanced in two heavy lines on the left, and, overlapping the Confederates, captured the redoubt, and appeared in the rear of the stonewall. The First had up to this time successfully held their ground against the attack in front, but now had to fall back, a considerable number being captured. Of Co. K, Moncrief was captured in the redoubt, and Sergt. Alexander, Corp. Rice and Private A. D. Ellis at the stonewall. T. M. Boggan, in attempting to leave the redoubt, was seriously wounded in the thigh and captured; he recovered from his wounds, and remained at Camp Chase till the war closed. Day, Killough, Martin and John Tunnell succeeded in escaping. The "First" was hotly engaged again on the 16th, and in the two days lost some 75 killed, wounded and prisoners.

The retreat from Tennessee abounds with incidents, but they belong either to the history of the army or to personal experience. Gen. Walthall commanded the rear-guard, of which Gen. Obdycke, the Northern officer who restored Schofield's broken lines at Franklin, says:—"The rear-guard remained firm, and did its work bravely to the last.... Walthall and Forrest selected one position after another with such unerring judgment that even Wilson and Wood were unable to gain any important advantage during a period of twelve days, and over a distance of 100 miles." As in the advance, so in the retreat, the ragged remnant of the First Alabama was always ready for duty—"faithful even unto death."

The following letter from Gen. E. C. Walthall to the writer testifies to their services:—

"Grenada, Miss., April 20, 1885.

"My Dear Sir:—Your letter written to me at Washington was mislaid but not forgotten. Gen. Quarles' brigade was with us on the retreat from Nashville, and the First Alabama Regiment was along. The rear-guard was composed of eight brigades, but they were all so small that I temporarily consolidated them in four. Quarles' and Featherston's were put in one, commanded by Gen. Featherston. The troops all behaved splendidly, and their services were all of great value.

"Your friend truly,
"E. C. Walthall."

Wounded men got out as best they could, many hobbling along the frozen pikes on crutches. Among these were all the members of Co. K wounded at Franklin. Shoal Creek, a stream swollen at that time to formidable proportions, seemed at one time to have cut off the retreat of the cripples, but kind-hearted cavalrymen carried those across who could not wade. It was nearly 100 yards wide, with a rocky bottom full of holes. In one instance, seen by the writer, a mule slipping threw a cripple into water nearly to his armpits; but the soldier held on to his crutches, and without assistance finally hobbled ashore. A cavalryman who had already carried several over returned, against the remonstrances of his companions, and took the writer across. The next morning, Saturday, December 24, the crowd of wounded men were ferried across the Tennessee in pontoon boats at a point near Florence, Ala., and were safe.

The First Alabama arrived at Verona, Miss., on January 16, 1865; thence they were ordered to report to Gen. Joseph E. Johnston, in North Carolina. Six of Co. K were with the regiment: Corp. Josiah Tunnell, Privates Griffin, Killough, Martin, Robinson and John Tunnell. The regiment, numbering about 100 men, participated in the last two battles of the war, Averysboro and Bentonville. On the last day of the second battle, at sundown, Lieut. William Williamson, Co. C, a gallant Christian gentlemen, was mortally wounded. The First Alabama was present, and ended its untarnished career at the surrender of Gen. Johnston's army at Greensboro', N. C., on the 27th of April, 1865. Those of Co. K present at the surrender arrived at Prattville about the middle or last of May, but it was about the 1st of July before all the scattered band got to their homes.

John Killough, John and Josiah Tunnell won the honorable distinction of being present when the company was mustered in and when it was disbanded. If the writer remembers correctly, the first two mentioned were never absent during the three years of service except when the main body of the regiment were prisoners of war or paroled. The last named of the three was also present except for two brief intervals, during one of which he was at the hospital, wounded.

Death, wounds, disease and imprisonment—the sad fortunes of war—kept others from sharing this honor.

# CHAPTER XII.

Prison Life during the Last Year of the War—Searching the Prisoners—Starvation Rations—True to the South—Home Again.


The following extract from a letter written by W. L. Ellis, Esq., conveys a vivid picture of the treatment of prisoners by the Federals during the last year of the war. Mr. Ellis was taken prisoner at Franklin.

"I surrendered to the Colonel of the Eighth Tennessee (U. S.) Regiment, and for kindness shown me by him I shall always feel very grateful. At midnight his command withdrew from the breastworks and started for Nashville, I accompanying him. We reached the hills near Nashville at daylight and halted for breakfast, of which I partook—and keenly enjoyed—with the Colonel. I remained with him till 5, P. M., Thursday, when, with 60 other prisoners, I was sent into Nashville. When our guards halted near the capitol, the prisoners asked for water, which a kind lady offered to bring, but the officer in charge refused permission. She was very indignant; but there was no redress, and we could only thank her heartily for her kind intentions. We were then escorted to the State prison and locked up for the night. Here a bit of bread and meat was handed us by a negro. At daylight we were put on a train for Louisville, where we arrived late in the evening, and were again locked up in prison, the negro guards giving each a small piece of bread and meat. Saturday morning we crossed the river and marched to the depot, where rations of baker's bread and ham were given us. After living on one meal a day, this food was very acceptable to the hungry prisoners. We then took the cars for Indianapolis, where we remained one hour. The citizens would have treated us very kindly had it not been for the officer in charge. It was here that a gentleman quietly informed us that if we had any currency, to conceal it, for we would be searched. His advice was, of course, taken by the fortunate few who had a dollar. The train arrived at Chicago about 1 o'clock Sunday morning, and we were ordered into line and marched three miles through a heavy snow, and then put into some old barracks, to remain without fire till the dawn of day. It was intensely cold, and it seemed impossible to keep from freezing. At daylight the prisoners were ordered into line, marched to the prison-gates of Camp

Douglas, halted and ordered to ground and unstrap knapsacks. After searching them thoroughly, and throwing out such articles as they chose, they ordered us to partly undress, that they might search our clothing for money. The search ended, we marched into the enclosure and were allotted to barracks. Soon after, an orderly came in and notified those without blankets to go with him to the Captain's office, and he would furnish them. Only three or four, of whom I was one, went. While waiting at the office-door my ears froze—it was so cold. I received a blanket and a pair of shoes.

"On the second day after our arrival, they appointed one of the prisoners 'Sergeant of the Barracks,' his duty being to call the roll and see that all was kept in proper order. The barracks were 18×48 feet, and to each were allotted 165 men. The prison-yard was said to contain 25 acres, and there were within the enclosure 59 barracks, 1 office and 1 sutler's store.

"Our rations consisted of two-thirds of a loaf of baker's bread, weighing ten ounces, and eight ounces of fresh beef, except on every tenth day, when we drew pork and beans. To divide the beans—they were so few—we had to count them, and the ration of pork amounted to almost nothing. The men suffered so from hunger that a prisoner would break the ice, and wash what we called an outfit—consisting of shirt, pants, drawers and socks— dry, and fold them ready for use, for five cents, with which he would buy a bit of bread. Prisoners from East Tennessee, Kentucky and Missouri could get money from home, and fared sumptuously as compared with those of us who lived south of the enemy's line. They were not permitted to receive the money, but were given sutler's tickets, which could be used at the store.

"I formed the acquaintance of two gentlemen, Messrs. Beel and Black, from Kentucky, who insisted upon my messing with them, and I fared much better than others, as my friends procured supplies from the sutler. We remained together two or three months, when, through the influence of friends, they were removed into what we called the 'loyal barracks.' There were hundreds of poor fellows who received nothing but their scanty rations, which barely kept them alive—in fact, I believe some died from starvation.

"The system of punishment was barbarous in the extreme. They had a wooden horse, made similar to a carpenter's saw-bench, twenty or twenty-five feet long and ten or twelve feet high, which they called a 'Morgan mule.' On this I have seen prisoners, as many as could be crowded on, remain six and eight hours in the cold and sleet. It appeared to me they would freeze to death. Another punishment was to make the offending prisoner stand in a bending position with his fingers in the snow as long as they saw fit. In each barracks there was one guard who appeared to have absolute authority to punish at will the prisoners under his charge. The barracks in which I bunked was more fortunate than many. Our guard was a gentlemanly fellow from Memphis named Nelson; he never punished a prisoner during my stay.

"Notwithstanding the treatment we received, we could not be driven to take the oath, but remained loyal to the Confederacy, having the utmost confidence in its triumph. The morning we received the news of the surrender of Gen. Lee, Gen. Sweet, the commandant of the prison, ordered us in line and left it to a vote whether we would have the United States flag hoisted in the prison yard; only two voted in favor of it. The guards were very angry and told the prisoners they ought to remain there always, but the flag was not hoisted. Soon after we received the news of the surrender of the other Confederate armies, and the work of paroling the prisoners was begun. I arrived home on June 18, 1865."

This evidence of Mr. Ellis is fully sustained by letters from Messrs. John C. Hearn and James D. Rice; the latter writes: "We fared very badly; the rations were very slim and the treatment was cruel indeed. I have seen many old men crying for something to eat." Mr. T. M. Boggan, who was at Camp Chase writes: "I was treated very well only our rations were rather short."

In closing this brief sketch of the services of Co. K, the author wishes to place on record that this has been a labor of love. There was not a comrade for whom he had not the kindliest regard; there was scarcely one to whom he was not indebted, during the three years, for some act showing a reciprocal feeling. For any shortcomings in this history he asks their lenient judgment, assuring each and every one that naught has been set down, naught omitted in malice. God bless the survivors of Co. K! God rest the souls of those whose ashes are scattered from the Lakes to the Gulf!

**THE END.**

# APPENDIX.

## ROLL OF CO. K, FIRST ALABAMA REGIMENT, C. S. A.

*The following is a complete roll of Co. K, First Alabama Regiment, C. S. A., with the highest rank attained, date of enlistment, County residence, and situation at the close of the war of each man.*

| NAMES. | RANK. | ENLISTED. | COUNTY RESIDENCE. | CLOSE OF WAR. | REMARKS. |
|---|---|---|---|---|---|
| Adams, Jesse | Private | Feb., 1863 | Mobile | | Mg., July 14, 1863. |
| Adams, N. K. | 2d Lieut. Jr. | Mar., 1862 | Montgomery | | Td. to C. S. N., July, 1864. |
| Alexander, J. L. | 1st Sergeant | Feb., 1863 | Autauga | Ab. Prisoner | Captured December 15, 1864. |
| Averheart, E. L. | Sergeant | Mar., 1862 | Autauga | Ab. Wounded | Wd. July 28 and November 30, 1864. |
| Blaylock, O. M. | Corporal | Mar., 1862 | Autauga | Ab. Wounded | Wd. July 28, 1864. |
| Boggan, John | Private | Feb., 1863 | Wilcox | Ab. Sick | Wd. July 28, 1864. |
| Boggan, T. M. | Private | Feb., 1863 | Wilcox | Ab. Prisoner | Wd. and Cap. December 15, 1864. |
| Boone, —— | Private | Feb., 1863 | Autauga | | Dd. June 29, 1863. |
| Bledsoe, G. R. | Private | Mar., 1862 | Coosa | | Td. to Eng. Corps, Jan., 1864. |
| Brown, A. P. Private | | Mar., 1862 | Autauga | | Dd. Sept. 24, 1862. |
| Brown, E. | Private | Mar., 1862 | Autauga | | Dd. Sept. 14, 1862. |
| Brown, C. W. | Private | Mar., 1862 | Autauga | | Wd. July 28, 1864. Kd. Nov. 30, 1864. |
| Byrd, J. H. | Private | Feb., 1863 | | | Dd. July 25, 1863. |
| Cameron, N. | Brvt. 1st Lieut. | Mar., 1862 | Autauga | | Kd. July 28, 1864. |

| Name | Rank | Enlisted | County | Remarks | Notes |
|---|---|---|---|---|---|
| Callens, R. H. | Private | Feb., 1863 | Butler | | Dd. Nov, 1863. |
| Clark, — — | Private | Feb., 1863 | Mobile | | Wd. May 10, 1863. Td. C. S. N., 1863. |
| Cook, J. N. | Private | Mar., 1862 | Autauga | | Dd. July 7, 1862. |
| Day, W. W. | Private | May, 1864 | Dallas | Ab. Sick | |
| Deno, M. | Private | Feb., 1863 | | | Mg. July 14, 1863. |
| Dennis, W. A. | Private | Mar., 1862 | Autauga | | Dd. Oct. 10, 1862. |
| Douglass, Wm. | Private | Feb., 1863 | | | Td. to C. S. N., Mar. 9, 1864. |
| Dubose, Wm. | Private | Feb., 1863 | Pike | | Kd. July 28, 1864. |
| Durden, G. W. | Private | Feb., 1863 | Autauga | Ab. Wounded | Wd. July 28, 1864. |
| Durden, J. H. | Private | Mar., 1862 | Autauga | Ab. Sick | |
| Ellis, A. D. | Private | Feb., 1864 | Autauga | Ab. Prisoner | Wd. June 19, 1864. Cap. Dec. 15, 1864. |
| Ellis, W. L. | Sergeant | Mar., 1862 | Autauga | Ab. Prisoner | Cap. Nov. 30, 1864. |
| Fay, Wm. H. | Sergeant | Mar, 1862 | Autauga | | Kd. Aug. 3, 1864. |
| Farmer, W. | Private | Mar., 1862 | Autauga | Ab. Sick | Wd. Aug. 3, 1864. |
| Fergerson, J. A. | Corporal | Mar., 1862 | Coosa | | Kd. May 27, 1863. |
| Fralick, H. | Private | Sept., 1862 | Autauga | | Td. March, 1864, to C. S. N. |
| Frank, John, Jr. | 2d Lieut. Jr. | Mar., 1862 | Autauga | | Kd. May 27, 1863. |
| Gibbons, G. W. | Private | May, 1864 | Autauga | Ab. Sick | |
| Glenn, Simeon | Private | Feb., 1863 | Autauga | | Dis. Oct. 21, 1864. |
| Golsan, P. G. | 2d Lieut. Jr. | Feb., 1863 | Autauga | | Kd. July 28, 1864. |
| Gorman, J. | Private | Feb., 1863 | | | Mg. July 22, 1864. |
| Gresham, A. F. | Private | June, 1864 | Escambia | | Dd. 1864. |
| Griffin, J. | Private | Mar., 1862 | Randolph | Present | |

| | | | | | |
|---|---|---|---|---|---|
| Hall, D. S. | 2d Lieut. | Mar., 1862 | Autauga | | Resigned Dec., 1862. |
| Hancock, M. M. | Private | Mar., 1862 | Autauga | | Dis. 1862. |
| Haley, — — | Private | Feb., 1863 | | | Mg. July 14, 1863. |
| Hamilton, J. | Private | Feb., 1863 | | | Mg. July 22, 1864. |
| Hearn, E. | Private | Mar., 1862 | Autauga | Ab. Wounded | Accidentally Wd. Nov. 29, 1864. |
| Hearn, G. W. | Sergeant | Mar., 1862 | Autauga | Ab. Prisoner | Cap. Oct. 5, 1864. |
| Hearn, J. C. | Private | Mar., 1862 | Autauga | Ab. Prisoner | Wd. July 28, 1864. Cap. Nov. 30, 1864. |
| Hern, M. | Private | Feb., 1863 | | | Mg. July 14, 1863. |
| Herndon, J. W. | Private | Mar., 1862 | Autauga | | Died July, 1863. |
| Hays, J. | Private | Feb., 1863 | | | Wd. May 27, 1863. Dd. Feb., 1864. |
| Holt, D. E. | Private | May, 1864 | Autauga | Ab. Wounded | Wd. Aug. 12, 1864. |
| Holston, J. G. | Private | Mar., 1862 | Autauga | Ab. Sick | Dd. July 6, 1863. |
| Hurd, Joseph | Private | Mar., 1862 | Autauga | Ab. Sick | |
| Hutchinson, W. H. | Corporal | Mar., 1862 | Autauga | | Td. to Cavalry. |
| Hunt, G. W. | Private | May, 1864 | Autauga | Ab. Sick | |
| Jenkins, E. | Private | Feb., 1863 | Pike | | Td. to C. S. N., Mar., 1864. |
| Killough, J. | Private | Mar., 1862 | Autauga | Present | |
| Kirkpatrick, R. H. | Private | Sept., 1863 | Butler | Ab. Sick | |
| Kirkpatrick, V. | Private | Feb., 1863 | Butler | Ab. Sick | |
| Lamar, M. D. | Sergeant | Feb., 1863 | Autauga | Ab. Wounded | Wd. July 28, 1864. |
| Leysath, E. | Private | Feb., 1863 | Butler | Ab. Wounded | Wd. July 28, 1864. |
| Lewis, J. | Private | Feb., 1863 | Montgomery | Ab. Sick | |
| Landers, N. | Private | June, 1864 | | Ab. Sick | |

| Name | Rank | Date | County | Status | Remarks |
|---|---|---|---|---|---|
| Martin, G. F. | Private | Feb., 1863 | Autauga | Present | Wd. Aug., 1864. |
| May, J. W. | Private | Mar., 1862 | Autauga | | Kd. Nov. 30, 1864. |
| Merritt, A. J. | Sergeant | Mar., 1862 | Autauga | | Dd. May 14, 1862. |
| Merritt, — — | Private | Feb., 1863 | | | Mg. July 14, 1863. |
| Mills, — — | Private | Feb., 1863 | | | Dd. July 5, 1863. |
| McCarty, J. | Private | Feb., 1863 | | | Kd. June 23d, 1863. |
| McDonald, — — | Private | Feb., 1863 | | | Dd. July, 1863. |
| Moncrief, C. J. | Private | Mar., 1862 | Autauga | | Dd. June, 1862. |
| Moncrief, Wm. | Private | Mar., 1862 | Autauga | Ab. Sick | |
| Owens, J. | Private | Feb., 1863 | Autauga | | Kd. July 28, 1864. |
| Pratt, M. E. | 1st Lieut. | Mar., 1862 | Autauga | Ab. Paroled | Wd. May 28, 1863. |
| Robinson, J. L. | Private | Mar., 1862 | Autauga | | Dis. April 1, 1862. |
| Robinson, Junius | Private | Mar., 1862 | Autauga | Present | |
| Roe, T. J. | Private | Mar., 1862 | Autauga | | Dd. May 9, 1862. |
| Rogers, J. C. | Sergeant | Mar., 1862 | Autauga | | Dis. 1864. |
| Royals, C. H. | Sergeant | Mar., 1862 | Autauga | Ab. Wounded | Wd. Nov. 30, 1864. |
| Royals, G. H. | Corporal | Mar., 1862 | Autauga | Ab. Sick | |
| Royals, J. M. | Corporal | Mar., 1862 | Autauga | | Dis. 1862. |
| Rice, J. D. | Corporal | Mar., 1862 | Autauga | Ab. Prisoner | Wd. July 4, 1864. Cap. Dec. 15, 1864. |
| Scott, B. L. | Private | Feb., 1863 | Autauga | | Dis. Oct. 21, 1864. |
| Scott, C. H. | Private | Feb., 1863 | Autauga | | Dd. July 3, 1863. |
| Sears, E. T. | Sergeant | Mar., 1862 | Autauga | | Dis. Sept., 1864. |
| Shaver, J. H. | Private | Feb., 1863 | Conecuh | | Wd. July 28, 1864. Dd. |

| Name | Rank | Enlisted | County | Remarks | |
| --- | --- | --- | --- | --- | --- |
| Simpson, J. L. | Private | Feb., 1863 | Butler | Ab. Wounded | Wd. July 28, 1864. |
| Shoals, J. | Private | Feb., 1863 | Montgomery | | Mg. July 14, 1863. |
| Schein, J. | Private | Feb., 1863 | | | Mg. July 14, 1863. |
| Smith, D. P. | 2d Lieut. Jr. | Mar., 1862 | Autauga | Ab. Wounded | Wd. Nov. 30, 1864. |
| Smith, M. A. | Private | Mar., 1862 | Autauga | | Dis. Mar. 25, 1862. |
| Smith, J. F. | Private | Mar., 1862 | Autauga | | Dd. May 15, 1862. |
| Smith, Henry | Private | Feb., 1863 | | | M. Wd. May 27, 1863. Dd. July 10. |
| Smyth, A. C. | Private | Feb., 1863 | Butler | | M. Wd. July 28, 1864. Dd. Aug. 14. |
| Stuart, J. J. | Private | Feb., 1863 | Wilcox | | M. Wd. July 28, 1864. Dd. Aug. |
| Tarleton, M. | Private | Feb., 1863 | Lowndes | | Dd. March 12, 1863. |
| Tarleton, John | Private | Mar., 1862 | Lowndes | | Dd. July, 1863. |
| Thompson, A. J. | Sergeant | Mar., 1862 | Autauga | | M. Wd. July 28, 1864. Dd. Aug. |
| Tharp, J. P. | Private | Feb., 1863 | | | Mg. July 21, 1864. |
| Trammell, W. M. | Private | June, 1864 | Tallapoosa | | Dd. 1864. |
| Tunnell, John S. | Private | Mar., 1862 | Autauga | Present | Wd. July 28, 1864. |
| Tunnell, Josiah | Corporal | Mar, 1862 | Autauga | Present | Wd. May 28, 1863, and Nov. 30, 1864. |
| Tuttle, C. E. | 2d Lieut. | Mar., 1862 | Montgomery | Ab. Prisoner | |
| Vaughn, W. | Private | Feb., 1863 | | Ab. Sick | |
| Ward, Isaac | Private | June, 1864 | Montgomery | Ab. Sick | |
| White, A. J. | Private | Feb., 1863 | Autauga | | Dd. July 25, 1863. |
| Whitfield, J. F. | Captain | Mar., 1862 | Montgomery | Ab. Prisoner | |
| Williamson, J. | Sergeant | Mar., 1862 | Autauga | Ab. Wounded | Wd. June, 1863, and July 28, 1864. |
| Wilkins, F. | Private | Mar., 1862 | Autauga | | Dis. 1864. |

| Wilson, T. A. | Private | Feb., 1863 | | Ab. Sick | |
| Winslett, —— | Private | Feb., 1863 | | | Kd. May 27, 1863. |

## *EXPLANATION OF ABBREVIATIONS.*

| | |
|---|---|
| Kd.—Killed. | Dis.—Discharged for disability. |
| Dd.—Died. | Cap.—Captured. |
| Wd.—Wounded. | Ab.—Absent. |
| M. Wd.—Mortally Wounded. | Td.—Transferred. |
| Mg.—Missing—fate unknown. | |

## *ROLL OF CO. K.*

The following is a summary of the roll of Co. K:—

| | | |
|---|--:|--:|
| Total enlisted and commissioned from March 1st to close of war | | 108 |
| Killed and mortally wounded | 15 | |
| Died of disease | 23 | |
| Missing, fate unknown | 10 | |
| Transferred to other service | 7 | |
| Discharged and resigned | 10 | —65 |
| Remaining on Roll at close of war | | 43 |
| Absent, wounded | 11 | |
| Absent, sick | 16 | |
| Absent, prisoners of war | 9 | |
| Absent on parole | 1 | —37 |
| Present for duty April 27, 1865 | | 6 |
| Number of men wounded once during the war | 24 | |
| Wounded twice | 3 | |
| Wounded and afterwards killed | 1 | |
| Total wounded | | 28 |
| Residence, from Autauga | 61 | |
| Butler | 6 | |
| Conecuh | 1 | |
| Coosa | 2 | |
| Dallas | 1 | |
| Escambia | 1 | |
| Lowndes | 2 | |
| Mobile | 2 | |
| Montgomery | 6 | |
| Pike | 2 | |
| Randolph | 1 | |
| Tallapoosa | 1 | |
| Wilcox | 3 | |
| Unknown | 19 | —108 |

Lector House believes that a society develops through a two-fold approach of continuous learning and adaptation, which is derived from the study of classic literary works spread across the historic timeline of literature records. Therefore, we aim at reviving, repairing and redeveloping all those inaccessible or damaged but historically as well as culturally important literature across subjects so that the future generations may have an opportunity to study and learn from past works to embark upon a journey of creating a better future.

This book is a result of an effort made by Lector House towards making a contribution to the preservation and repair of original ancient works which might hold historical significance to the approach of continuous learning across subjects.

HAPPY READING & LEARNING!

**LECTOR HOUSE LLP**
E-MAIL: lectorpublishing@gmail.com

www.ingramcontent.com/pod-product-compliance
Lightning Source LLC
LaVergne TN
LVHW090009200726
843493LV00004B/832